RESEARCH REPORT SEPTEMBER 2015

Suspending Chicago's Students

Differences in Discipline Practices across Schools

Lauren Sartain, Elaine M. Allensworth, and Shanette Porter
with Rachel Levenstein, David W. Johnson, Michelle Hanh Huynh, Eleanor Anderson, Nick Mader, and Matthew P. Steinberg

TABLE OF CONTENTS

ACKNOWLEDGEMENTS

We are grateful to the Chicago Public Schools (CPS) for assisting us in conducting this study, for sharing their insights into school practices around discipline, and for providing the administrative data that allowed us to do this work—particularly Karen van Ausdal, Justina Schlund, and the Office of Social and Emotional Learning. We are very thankful for CPS administrators and teachers who took the time to share their experiences with discipline in their school buildings. We thank our Steering Committee members for their thoughtful comments, in particular Lila Leff and Chris Jones, for reading the report thoroughly. This report benefited from feedback from our fellow researchers at the University of Chicago Consortium on Chicago School Research (UChicago CCSR), in particular Camille Farrington and Josh Klugman. UChicago CCSR communications team members, especially Bronwyn McDaniel and Jessica Puller, provided assistance in publishing this report. Lucinda Fickel of the Urban Education Institute was also instrumental in the release of this report. Valerie Michelman also participated in instrumental meetings that significantly improved this report. The Atlantic Philanthropies provided generous funding for this line of research, which made this report possible. Finally, we also gratefully acknowledge the Spencer Foundation and the Lewis-Sebring Family Foundation, whose operating grants support the work of UChicago CCSR.

This report was produced by UChicago CCSR's publications and communications staff: Bronwyn McDaniel, Director for Outreach and Communication; and Jessica Puller, Communications Specialist.

Graphic Design: Jeff Hall Design
Photography: Cynthia Howe
Editing: Ann Lindner

09.2015/pdf/jh.design@rcn.com

Executive Summary

School districts across the country, including the Chicago Public Schools (CPS), are implementing policies aimed at reducing suspensions. The district has initiated a number of reforms over the past six years to bring about changes in schools' disciplinary practices with the goal of reducing the use of suspensions, as well as disparities in suspension rates by students' race, gender, and disability status. This report shows that a subset of schools drive high suspension rates, and these schools serve concentrations of extremely disadvantaged students.

The first report in this series showed that out-of-school suspension (OSS) and arrest rates have been going down since 2009-10 in Chicago's schools, but that racial and gender disparities remain large. African American students are about three times more likely to be suspended than Latino students, and more than four times more likely to be suspended than white or Asian students. Boys are much more likely to be suspended than girls of the same race/ethnicity.

This report looks more closely at differences in the suspension and arrests rates based on students' background characteristics. It also shows differences in the use of suspensions across schools in Chicago and the degree to which schools' use of suspensions is related to the learning climate of the school and student achievement. Identifying the schools that use exclusionary discipline practices at extremely high rates can help districts target supports and interventions to the schools that need them the most, rather than relying on a district-wide, one-size-fits-all approach.

Key Findings

Students with the most vulnerable backgrounds are much more likely to be suspended than students without those risk factors. Almost a third of the high school students who were at some point victims of abuse or neglect were suspended in the 2013-14 school year. Over a quarter of the high school students from the poorest neighborhoods and over a quarter of students with the lowest incoming achievement were suspended during the year. The students that come to school the furthest behind also are the most likely to miss instructional time due to a suspension.

At the same time, differences in the suspension rates for students with different risk factors, such as poverty and low achievement, do not explain most of the large racial and gender disparities in suspension rates. While African American students are more likely to face these problems, these background factors do not explain most of the differences in suspension rates by race. There are large disparities in suspension rates by race and by gender, even among students who have none of these risk factors.

The biggest driver of racial disparities in suspension rates comes from differences in which schools students of different races/ethnicities attend. Racial disparities in suspensions could exist for multiple reasons. There could be differences in suspension rates among students who attend the same school, or students of different races could attend schools with very different suspension rates. We see evidence for both of these in Chicago's schools, although it is school differences in suspension rates that drive most of the racial disparities.

Suspension rates are twice as high, on average, at the schools attended by African American students than the schools attended by Latino students, and the average suspension rates at the schools attended by Latino students are more than twice as high as the average suspension rates at the schools that white and Asian students attend. Because residential segregation leads schools in Chicago to be very segregated by race, differences in suspension rates across schools lead to differences in suspension rates by race.

Differences in suspension rates among subgroups of students within schools also exist, although they are modest relative to the differences in average suspension rates across schools. The largest difference occurs for African American boys, who are suspended at much higher rates than other students *in the same school.* At schools that are racially/ethnically diverse, suspension rates of African American boys are 11-12 percentage points higher than their school average. At the same time, Latina, white, and Asian girls are suspended at lower rates than their school classmates, with average suspension rates that are 3-5 percentage points below other students at their schools.

The extent to which schools rely on disciplinary practice is strongly correlated with the characteristics of the students in the school. Schools across Chicago vary considerably in the backgrounds of the students they serve. While almost all schools in the district serve high proportions of students from low-income backgrounds, and would be considered *"high-poverty"* schools compared to national averages, they differ considerably in the degree of poverty and their students' incoming academic skills. Strong residential segregation, by race and economic, is compounded by sorting based on academic skills, particularly at the high school level where students apply to selective schools and programs based on their academic performance in the middle grades. In fact, there is almost no overlap in the student body characteristics of high schools with low suspension rates compared to high schools with high suspension rates. In the middle grades there is some overlap in the student body composition of schools with high and low suspension rates, but the relationships of suspension rates with students' prior achievement and neighborhood poverty are still very strong.

Many CPS schools have low suspension rates. About a third of high schools, and three-fourths of schools serving the middle grades, have low rates of suspensions and other exclusionary disciplinary practices. Students of all racial/ethnic backgrounds, boys and girls, are unlikely to be suspended at these schools. All schools that serve students with high incoming achievement have low suspension rates.

It is the concentration of many low-achieving students from high-poverty neighborhoods that seems to increase the likelihood that a school will have high suspension rates. Almost all of these schools have predominantly African American students. About one-quarter of high schools, and 10 percent of schools serving the middle grades, assign out-of-school suspensions to a third or more of their students each year. At many of these schools half of the students receive an OSS in a year. These schools also have the highest rates of in-school suspensions and arrests at school, and they tend to give out the longest suspensions. The suspension practices at these schools, coupled with the fact that they serve African American students, drive the racial/ethnic disparities at the district level. Furthermore, at the high school level, at least 1 in 10 students at these schools has a confirmed history of having been abused or neglected, though all students are at high risk of suspension in these schools—even students with no prior risk factors.

Schools with the highest suspension rates have climates that are the least conducive for learning. The schools that extensively use exclusionary discipline practices tend to serve very disadvantaged students who most need a very supportive environment. Yet, by attending these schools, students not only are at high risk of being suspended and missing instruction, but they also experience poor climates for instruction. The climate for learning is much worse in schools with high rates of exclusionary disciplinary practices, even when comparing schools serving similar student populations. Teachers report more crime and disorder in buildings with high suspension rates, and students are much more negative about peer relationships and safety in these same schools.

Shortening the length of suspensions has mixed consequences for schools—better attendance but worse climate, and no impact on test scores. In interviews, school staff described conflicted feelings about suspensions—they felt that getting disruptive students out of the school and classroom helped to maintain order and improved the instructional climate, but they noted that the suspension could cause the student being punished to fall behind and have worse behavioral problems in the future. This suggests that suspensions might simultaneously have mixed consequences for schools. In fact, we found this to be the case. After the introduction of the CPS policy to reduce the length of suspensions, student attendance went up by about a week in high-suspending high schools. However, student and teacher reports of school climate worsened after implementation of the policy. Test scores, which prior research has shown to be influenced both by attendance and by school climate, remained the same. Thus, there seem to be trade-offs that come from mandating shorter suspensions—teachers need better supports and strategies to maintain order while keeping students in the classroom so that they do not fall behind.

The schools with the most suspensions are also trying different solutions to address behavioral issues, but they may be too inundated to be successful. Suspensions alone may be unlikely to improve disciplinary problems without additional measures for addressing students' misbehavior. However, half of suspensions are given without being accompanied by additional strategies—including parent conferences or restorative justice practices. At the same time, evidence for supplementing suspensions with other practices is mixed—only showing potential benefits in schools with low or moderate suspension rates. Unfortunately, the quality of data records on discipline practices does not allow for an analysis of practices that do not accompany a suspension. There is a need for much better data around discipline practices in schools to understand what is effective.

This report highlights substantial challenges for schools that serve students with the most vulnerable backgrounds. In those schools where large proportions of the student body come to school with low academic achievement levels, high poverty, and prior family stress, there are more demands on school staff to maintain a safe, orderly, and academically focused climate. Yet, simply reducing the time students are suspended, or requiring parent conferences or the use of restorative practices along with suspensions, may bring other challenges. Changing practices will take substantial support and resources to do well in schools serving students from the most disadvantaged neighborhoods, along with school leadership committed to substantially changing practices and reducing discipline disparities for students in their schools.

College & Career Resource Center
Friday, May 16, 2014
The Fabulous Naturals
FREE ADMISSION

Introduction

School districts across the country are in the midst of a fundamental shift in how they approach discipline in schools, moving away from *"zero tolerance"* discipline policies that result in high rates of student suspensions. These changes have emerged out of concerns that exclusionary discipline practices are ineffective for improving student behavior and school climate, and may even lead to worse outcomes for students and a more problematic school environment for learning.

Studies have shown that even small amounts of absence can have substantial long-term consequences on educational attainment.[1] Further, students who are expelled or suspended are more likely to fail courses, repeat grades, and drop out of school than other students.[2] Policy statements from the American Academy of Pediatrics, American Psychological Association, and American Bar Association have come out strongly against the over-use of suspensions, noting negative educational, social, and health consequences that are perceived to result from the punishments themselves.[3]

However, changing disciplinary practices in schools is not easy. Schools need to address misbehavior to maintain a safe and orderly climate, and suspending students has been a standard response to misbehavior in schools for many years. While removing students from instruction could impede learning for those students, school staff worry that keeping disruptive or threatening students in the classroom can impede the learning of all other students. To help staff rely less on suspensions for addressing disciplinary issues, many schools are adopting alternative approaches that often incorporate programs to help students develop better conflict management skills and group or one-on-one counseling.

Chicago Public Schools (CPS) has increasingly encouraged the use of non-exclusionary disciplinary practices in schools. District policies have included funding for implementing alternative programs for addressing behavioral problems, as well as modifications to the CPS Student Code of Conduct (SCC), to discourage schools from using suspensions and reduce the amount of time students miss school when they are suspended. CPS has adopted a Multi-Tiered System of Supports (MTSS),[4] also known as Response to Intervention, to help guide the use of various alternative discipline approaches depending on the needs of individual students, from prevention of disciplinary practices across all students, to targeted supports for students with higher needs, to individualized interventions for students with severe needs. A number of schools have implemented programs that teach students positive behaviors (e.g., Positive Behavior Interventions and Support, known as PBIS), or address social-emotional learning. PBIS has been found in prior research to reduce office disciplinary referrals and suspensions while improving peer

1 Allensworth & Easton (2007); Allensworth, Gwynne, Moore, & de la Torre (2014).
2 Fabelo et al. (2011); Balafanz, Byrnes, & Fox (2015).
3 American Academy of Pediatrics (2003); American Psychological Association Zero Tolerance Task Force (2008); American Bar Association (2001).
4 Accessed from https://sites.google.com/site/cpspositivebehavior/home/about-positive-behavior-supports/strategies

relationships, increasing instructional time, and improving student reports of safety.[5] For students who are facing disciplinary action, many schools are implementing restorative justice programs, where students are taught to take responsibility and repair harm, rather than simply receiving a suspension or other punishment. Some schools that use restorative justice programs also see a decline in suspensions, expulsions, and violent behaviors.[6]

Concurrent with these efforts, there have been lower rates of out-of-school suspensions and arrests at school. In March 2015, we released a study showing that out-of-school suspension (OSS) rates and arrests at school have been declining since 2010. At the same time, students and teachers reported feeling safer at their schools.[7] Despite these changes, the report also showed that suspension rates were still very high among CPS high school students, especially among some subgroups of students. In fact, 33 percent of African American boys in high school were suspended in the 2013-14 school year.

In this report, we look further into racial and gender disparities in the use of suspensions in CPS to understand the extent to which schools across the city, serving different groups of students, use suspensions at high rates, and some of the factors that underlie large disparities. We examine suspensions among students in grades 6-12 in the 2013-14 school year, which comes after five years of CPS policies aimed at reducing the use of suspensions and increasing reliance on restorative practices. We focus on out-of-school suspensions, but also examine other exclusionary discipline practices—those that take students out of the classroom and exclude them from instruction—such as in-school suspension (ISS) and arrest. (**See box entitled *Definitions of Key Terms* on p.10** for more information on exclusionary and non-exclusionary practices.) We also show the extent to which schools accompany suspensions with other interventions, such as conferences with parents, the use of restorative practices, or conferences with counselors.

In the first report, we showed that high school suspensions make up over half of out-of-school suspensions in the district, as well as the vast majority of in-school suspensions and arrests at school. Therefore, we primarily examine the use of exclusionary discipline practices in high schools, and then compare patterns of suspension usage in the middle grades in a final chapter.

Research Questions

The report addresses five main questions:

1. **What drives disparities in suspension rates in the district—differences by students' backgrounds within schools, or differences in general practices across schools?**

   The first report in this series showed that there are large disparities in the exclusionary disciplinary practices by students' race and gender. This report explores those differences to understand why they exist. One possible explanation is that differences in suspension rates are due to other differences between students—their achievement level, neighborhood poverty, or other difficult circumstances that might also be related to disparities in suspension rates. Another explanation is that students from some groups are more likely to be suspended than other students in their school, and there is research that suggests school personnel are more likely to suspend minority boys than girls or non-minority students.[8] A final explanation is that suspension rates are driven by differences in the general practices of the schools that they attend, with students from some groups more likely to attend schools that use exclusionary practices more often than other schools. Chapter 1 shows that there is some evidence that is consistent with each of these three potential explanations. However, it is differences *between* schools in their overall use of suspensions that drive the majority of the racial disparities and some of the gender disparities. Chapter 2, therefore, looks in-depth at differences across schools in the use of exclusionary practices.

5 LaFrance (2009); Lassen, Steele, & Sailor (2006).
6 Stinchcomb et al. (2006).
7 Stevens, Sartain, Allensworth, & Levenstein (2015).
8 Fabelo et al. (2011); Losen & Gillepsie (2012); Losen & Martinez (2013); Losen, Hewitt, & Toldson (2014); Stevens et al. (2015).

2. In what ways do schools differ in their use of exclusionary discipline practices?

Administrators at individual schools are charged with maintaining order and securing a safe environment for students, and they must decide what is best for the students and staff in their school. Those decisions at individual schools lead to the system-wide patterns that are observed. This report unpacks system-wide trends to focus on disciplinary practices across schools—showing differences in the ways in which schools are using exclusionary practices, especially suspensions, and how these differences vary by the types of students the school serves. If most schools have similar suspension rates, it suggests a very different strategy for changing disciplinary practices than if there are large differences from school to school. In fact, Chapter 2 shows that there are a contained number of schools that have particularly high rates of exclusionary disciplinary practices. It also shows that these schools serve students who begin the year the farthest behind academically and many students who come from very vulnerable backgrounds—students who most need a safe and supportive school environment.

3. How is the use of exclusionary practices related to school climate and student learning?

Schools relying on suspensions are less safe and orderly than schools serving similar populations of students that suspend students much less frequently.[9] However, it is difficult to determine whether suspensions lead to a decline in school learning climate, or whether schools with poor climates simply have a greater need to punish students—leading to more suspensions. Chapter 3 shows how school climate is different in schools using exclusionary discipline to different degrees. It replicates the relationships observed in the past with more recent data and considers a larger array of student background factors, showing that school learning climate is worse in schools with higher suspension rates, even when comparing schools serving similar populations of students. It then shows what happened when the district policy forced schools to limit the number of days that students were suspended: mixed consequences for students and schools.

4. To what extent are suspensions accompanied by supplemental supportive practices, and are these practices related to school climate?

The first report in this series showed that the vast majority of suspensions came about because students disobeyed a teacher or broke school rules, with many suspensions also resulting from fights among students. Thus, reducing the use of exclusionary practices would seem to require ways to build better relationships between students and their teachers, and among students in the school. Some schools have received resources to train staff and students in restorative practices, where students learn to take responsibility for their behavior and build skills for handling future problems. Peer juries, for example, bring together a student who has broken a school rule with trained student jurors to discuss why the incident occurred, who was affected, and how the student can repair the harm he/she caused. Alternatively, school staff might call a conference with parents, or set up times for the student to meet with the school counselor to identify and address underlying issues. Yet, Chapter 4 shows that only about half of suspensions are accompanied by a supplemental practice intended to improve subsequent behavior. Furthermore, it is not clear how beneficial such supplemental practices are when they occur—particularly in schools with high suspension rates.

5. How do discipline practices in the middle grades differ from high school?

In this report, we show that the high suspension rates in CPS high schools are driven by a group of high schools that serve really struggling student populations. The fact that these high-suspend-

9 Steinberg, Allensworth, & Johnson (2011).

ing high schools overwhelmingly serve African American students helps to explain the racial disparities in suspension rates in the district. One question that arises is whether or not this is a high school problem. Chapter 5 contrasts the use of exclusionary discipline practices in the middle grades and high schools, showing the variation in suspension and arrest rates across schools that serve middle grades students and characterizing the schools with the highest rates of these exclusionary practices. While the same general patterns emerge among students in the middle grades as among students in high school, the suspension rates are lower and the relationships between suspension rates and the types of students served by schools are less stark. At the high school level, there is no overlap in the characteristics of the student body served by schools with high versus low suspension rates; in the middle grades there are schools with low suspension rates serving all types of students. However, as with high schools, the schools with the highest suspension rates all serve the most vulnerable student populations.

Data Limitations Create Barriers to Understanding Discipline Practices in Schools

Understanding the ways in which schools address discipline problems—and the effects of those practices on school climate and instruction—requires consistently recorded data on the disciplinary incidents that occur in schools and the responses that schools take to those incidents. While there are systems and procedures set up to record that information, analysis of the data suggests that only incidents that result in a student receiving a suspension or an arrest are recorded regularly at schools.[10] Because there is no way of reliably knowing how often infractions occurred in schools other than those accompanied by suspensions, we are unable to study the effects of replacing suspensions with other forms of intervention, or whether the overall rate of infractions has decreased due to prevention efforts in schools. Thus, this study focuses on the use of suspensions in schools—the degree to which schools use suspensions and the relationship of the use of suspensions with school climate and instruction.

There are a number of issues that impede the collection of consistent data on disciplinary infractions and school responses:

- Historically, there was little incentive for schools to record information unless required as part of the documentation for a suspension. Even though the district is now encouraging better documentation and has clearer guidelines and a revised data system, there are substantial barriers to documentation at the school level. It takes time and personnel to record data, and the people who enter the information need to have training to enter it consistently. There may need to be regular review of the data to make sure it is being entered accurately, and that it represents what is actually occurring at the school.
- It is not always clear when an incident warrants entry into the data—reporting can vary from one school to the next, or even across classrooms in the same school. Many of the disciplinary responses that occur in a school are informal and likely are not officially recorded—a teacher sits a student in the hallway during class, or talks with a student after class; an administrator admonishes a student for running in the hall. There is discretion at the school level in how school personnel handle misbehavior, so it is possible that an infraction would be officially recorded at one school and dealt with informally at another school. If incidents of this nature are recorded at another school, the official records may make two similar schools look very different in terms of level of misbehavior just because one school chooses to record and another does not.
- There is inconsistency in the terminology used for practices across schools. For example, *"peace circles"*

10 Almost all disciplinary incidents that are recorded in the administrative records include a response of a suspension (87 percent include a suspension). Furthermore, it is rare for low-level types of infractions—those that are not considered serious enough to warrant a suspension—to appear in the misconduct files, even though it is likely that those types of infractions actually occur much more frequently than high-level infractions.

and *"restorative chats"* are used under a restorative justice framework in response to a specific disciplinary incident as an alternative or supplement to suspension. However, these terms are also sometimes used to refer to talking circles intended to prevent disciplinary incidents from occurring, or to address low-level tensions before they escalate. *"Parent conferences"* could refer to many different types of contact, from collaborative to antagonistic, face-to-face or by phone, focused on support or punishment, and with very different consequences for building relationships among adults and with the student. In addition, schools may give punishments that seem similar to suspensions, but that go by another name—such as *"in-school detention"* instead of *"in-school suspension."* It is not possible to tell from the administrative data the nature of these different types of punishments.

Thus, there are a number of barriers to studying how schools respond to student misbehavior and, especially, the effects of alternative discipline practices. The district has invested considerable resources into changing schools' disciplinary practices; but without good data about what is happening with the implementation of those practices, it is not possible to know their effects. The one area with which we can study school disciplinary practices with sufficient confidence in the data is around their use of exclusionary practices, particularly the use of suspensions. Given the goals of the district around decreasing the use of suspensions, and the concern locally and nationally with the racial disparities in suspension rates, this is a critical issue itself. However, because of these limitations, we can only present a partial examination of disciplinary practices in Chicago schools.

Data Sources and Years

Data for this report come from a number of sources, including CPS and Department of Child and Family Services (DCFS) administrative data, student and teacher responses to the *My Voice, My School* surveys, and interviews with administrators and teachers.

Exclusionary Discipline Practices (Suspensions & Arrests)

Information about schools' use of suspensions and police are derived from CPS misconduct data on infractions, suspensions, and police involvement. These data indicate when a student is suspended, for what infraction, and for how many days. There is also information on additional supports a school provided to a student to accompany a suspension. We do not include students enrolled in charter, alternative, or special education schools, as this information is inconsistently recorded in these schools. The findings presented in Chapters 1 and 2 use data from the 2013-14 school year. Analysis of the effect of reducing suspensions on learning and school climate in Chapter 3 uses administrative and survey data from 2010-11 to 2013-14. All data sources are described further in **Appendix A.**

Supplemental Supports

Supportive practices are identified from CPS misconduct data (described above) from the 2013-14 school year. When a student is suspended, schools must report additional supports provided to the student, such as a parent conference. (**See Appendix B** for options that schools can indicate.) Data presented here do not include students enrolled in charter, alternative, or special education schools, as described in **Appendix A**.

Measures of School Climate

Student and teacher perceptions of safety and climate come from district-wide *My Voice, My School* surveys from the springs of 2011-14. We do not include charter, alternative, or special education schools in analyses that compare school climate with discipline practices since we do not have consistent data from these schools on discipline practices. For more information on the survey, **see Appendix C**.

Interviews with Administrators and Teachers

We also use information from two waves of interview data collection: **1)** 20 administrator interviews conducted for this study in the spring and early summer of 2013 in ten elementary schools and ten high schools and **2)** 30 school personnel interviews that took place in spring and summer of 2014 in three elementary schools and two high schools. Data from the first round of interviews are interwoven in the text, while the case studies from the second round of interviews are highlighted in boxes. **See Appendix A** for details about sampling and analysis methods.

Definitions of Key Terms

CPS Student Code of Conduct (SCC): This document outlines what behaviors are inappropriate for students and the appropriate ways for schools to address misbehavior. It is modified annually and parents and students are required to sign it. The SCC requires mandatory suspensions of varying lengths for some offenses, while leaving room for school discretion in handling other, less serious offenses. The most recent version of the SCC can be accessed at **http://cps.edu/Pages/StudentCodeofConduct.aspx**

Exclusionary Discipline Practices (EDP): Practices that result in the removal of students from the classroom, including out-of-school and in-school suspensions, as well as arrests. In this report we divide schools into three categories, based on the extent to which they use exclusionary disciplinary practices: low, medium, and high. **Appendix D** provides information about how schools were classified into these categories:

- **Low EDP Schools:** On average, fewer than 10 percent of students receive an OSS in a year, and almost no students are arrested at school; few receive an ISS.
- **Medium EDP Schools:** On average, about 20 percent of students receive an OSS in a year, about 1 percent are arrested at school; at the high school level, about 15 percent receive an ISS, on average.
- **High EDP Schools:** In the middle grades, on average, about a third of students receive an OSS in a year, and about 1.5 percent are arrested at school. In the high school grades, on average, about 40 percent of students receive an OSS and about 45 percent receive an ISS, while about 3 percent are arrested at school in a year.

Expulsion: A strategy that schools can also use to remove extremely disruptive students from the building. A student recommended for expulsion participates in a hearing where an officer determines if the student's actions are so disruptive or threatening that no alternative measure exists to address the behavior. These events are rare, so we do not include them in this report; CPS publicly reports that 351 high school students and 82 middle grades students were expelled in 2013-14.

Out-of-School Suspension (OSS): A disciplinary response that removes a student from the building for a set number of days.

In-School Suspension (ISS): A disciplinary response that removes a student from the classroom, but not from the building. Students sit in a room designated for in-school suspensions, or a make-shift space like a hallway or the main office, where they are expected to do schoolwork or sit quietly.

Police Involvement: CPS misconduct data indicate if a behavioral infraction resulted in police notification or arrest.

Suspension and Arrest Rates: We define rates as the percentage of students who experience a particular exclusionary practice in a given school year. For example, in 2013-14 the OSS rate for high school students was 16 percent—as we define it, this means that 16 percent of high school students received at least one OSS in the 2013-14 school year. Arrest rates include only arrests made during the school year, not made during the summer.

Supplemental Supports: These are non-exclusionary discipline practices that seek to change behaviors or offer behavioral supports to students, such as restorative practices, counseling, social-emotional training, and individualized interventions. These practices can be used in conjunction with exclusionary practices or in isolation. In this report, we only describe non-exclusionary practices that accompany suspensions.

Parent Conferences: These practices include any communication with a parent, such as a phone call or an in-person meeting.

Restorative Practices: These practices involve all parties who were involved in some kind of incident; participants talk about what happened and how they were affected, and they work together to find a resolution. Examples include peace circles, peer juries, and restorative conversations.

Individualized Interventions: These interventions target specific students and rely on assessment for personalized treatment. Examples include one-on-one counseling with a school psychologist or social worker or customized instruction plans.

CHAPTER 1

What Drives Disparities in Suspension Rates in High Schools?

The first report in this series, *Trends in the Use of Suspensions and Arrests*, showed that suspension rates in Chicago schools have historically been very high, but that they have declined in recent years. In 2009-10, about a quarter of high school students received an out-of-school suspension (OSS) each year. Suspension rates have declined since then, such that 16 percent of high school students received an OSS in the 2013-14 school year. At the same time, large disparities in suspension rates remain between African American students and students of other races, as well as between male and female students.

African American students in CPS are more likely to be suspended than students of other races/ethnicities, and boys are more likely to be suspended than girls. **Figure 1** shows OSS rates by race/ethnicity and gender in 2013-14. African American students' suspension rates are at least three times higher than the suspension rates of Latino students of the same gender, while white and Asian students are about half as likely to be suspended as Latino students. Boys are also more likely than girls of the same race/ethnicity to be suspended. Details about how these differences have changed over time are available in the first report.

FIGURE 1

There Are Large Differences in Suspension Rates for Students of Different Races/Ethnicities and Genders

Out-of-School Suspension Rates by Race/Ethnicity and Gender (High School Students, 2013-14)

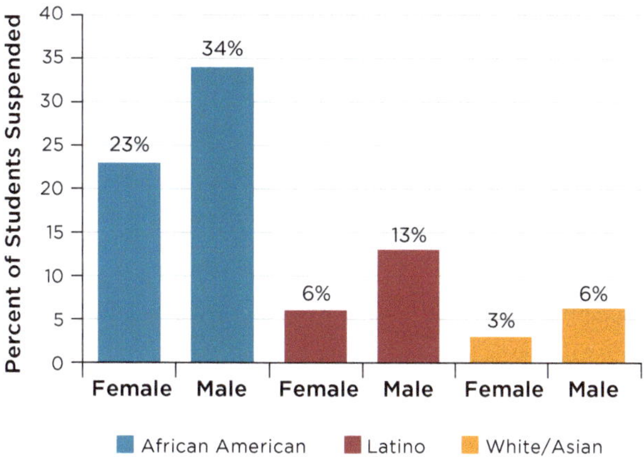

Note: When calculating suspension rates, the numerator is the total number of students in a subgroup (e.g., African American students in high school) assigned a suspension in that school year and the denominator is the total student enrollment for that subgroup. There are 17,501 African American female students; 15,766 African American male students; 19,273 Latina students; 19,674 Latino students; 6,507 white or Asian female students; and 6,513 white or Asian male students.

African American boys are also the student group most likely to be subject to other exclusionary discipline practices, like in-school suspensions and arrests. African American boys were much more likely to be arrested at school than any other students, with rates that were twice as high as Latino boys or African American girls, and four times higher than Latina, white, or Asian girls or white or Asian boys.

The Most Vulnerable Students, Who Come to School with the Greatest Challenges, Are the Most Likely to Be Suspended

Students are often struggling with hard issues outside of the school building. Some live in neighborhoods with very high rates of poverty. Some may be coping with stresses associated with a lack of family or neighborhood resources. Some students have faced particularly difficult issues in childhood; in fact, thousands of CPS students have at some time in their lives been victims of a substantiated case of abuse or neglect. Many students enter school with very low levels of academic achievement, making it difficult for them to reach the academic goals that have been set by their schools or teachers. Still other students have identified disabilities that can make school more difficult, even with appropriate supports. All of these students are much more likely to be suspended than students without these risk factors.

Figure 2 contrasts OSS rates of students who enter the school year with the most disadvantaged backgrounds to students who do not face those same risk factors. The most disadvantaged students are much more likely to be suspended than students who are less vulnerable. For example, in the 2013-14 school year, 27 percent of high

FIGURE 2

Students from More Vulnerable Backgrounds Are More Likely to Be Suspended than Other Students

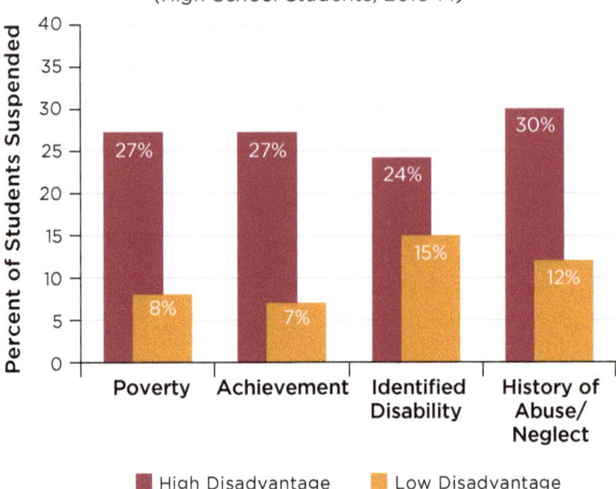

Note: When calculating suspension rates, the numerator is the total number of students in a subgroup (e.g., students who live in high-poverty neighborhoods) assigned at least one suspension in that school year and the denominator is the total student enrollment for that subgroup. High poverty is defined as students living in census block groups in the highest poverty quartile, relative to other students in the district at their grade level. Poverty is measured using U.S. Census data of the percentage of males unemployed and the percentage of families living under poverty in the census block group (which is about one city block in size). The contrast is students in the bottom quartile on the neighborhood poverty measure (i.e., the most affluent neighborhoods). Low achievement is similarly the lowest-performing quartile of students in their grade level based on the incoming reading and math test scores (scores from the prior year), contrasted with students in the top quartile on tests. Students with an identified disability have an IEP, excluding 504s, in the 2013-14 school year, contrasted with students without an IEP. Students with a history of abuse/neglect are students who have a substantiated allegation of abuse or neglect in the Child Abuse and Neglect Tracking System (CANTS) of the Illinois Department of Children and Family Services at any point in their life prior to the end of the 2013-14 school year, contrasted to students without a record of having been abused or neglected. The number of high school students in the High Disadvantage groups are 21,066 (poverty); 17,886 (achievement); 11,841 (disability); and 4,985 (abuse/neglect).

school students living in the poorest neighborhoods in Chicago were given an OSS. By contrast, about 8 percent of high school students from the neighborhoods with the lowest levels of poverty (the bottom quartile) received an OSS during the 2013-14 school year.[11]

This pattern is similar when comparing suspension rates by incoming achievement. More than a quarter of the lowest-achieving high school students (27 percent) received an OSS compared to 7 percent of the highest-achieving students (those in the bottom and top quartile of incoming achievement, respectively). Though the gap is less large for high school students with an identified disability, it is still present: 24 percent of high school students with an identified disability were suspended compared to 15 percent of high school students without an identified disability.

Students who have had a confirmed case of abuse or neglect at some point in their lives have the highest rate of suspension. Nearly a third of high school students (30 percent) with a reported history of abuse or neglect received an OSS, compared to 12 percent of high school students without a prior confirmed history of abuse or neglect.

High suspension rates among students who come to school the most behind and from the most vulnerable backgrounds are concerning. These students are most in need of instructional support while at school; however, the high risk of receiving an OSS means they are more likely than other students to miss instruction due to a suspension and have the potential to fall farther behind their classmates.

Disparities in Suspension Rates Come from Different Sources

The existence of large differences in suspension rates by students' background characteristics leads to questions about why there are disparities. Many factors could contribute to disparities in discipline outcomes. In this chapter, we investigate each of the following potential explanations for disparities in suspension rates:

1. Background characteristics—such as poverty and prior achievement—could underlie disparities associated with race and gender. Disparities in suspension rates might exist, in part, because of other differences in students' backgrounds that are correlated with race and gender—like poverty and academic performance. For example, African American students are more likely to live in the poorest neighborhoods in the city than Latino, white, or Asian students, and poverty may introduce stress that spills over into school environments.

11 High poverty is defined as living in a neighborhood where unemployment among males is high and most families live below the poverty line. These neighborhoods are in the top quartile in terms of poverty among all of the neighborhoods in which CPS students live.

2. Student groups could be treated differently at the same school. Schools might have policies that—intentionally or unintentionally—affect some students more than others. Some student groups may break rules more often, or school staff may hold biases that result in harsher punishments for some groups of students.[12] Biased perceptions or policies that result in some students being suspended at greater rates than others could be reflected in differences in suspension rates between student subgroups who attend the same school.
3. Student groups could attend schools with different overall suspension rates. In addition, schools could differ in their overall use of exclusionary practices, so that all students at some schools are at higher risk of suspension than students at other schools. To the extent that students of different races and genders attend schools with higher or lower suspension rates, differences across schools in their use of suspensions could result in greater suspension of some groups than others. In CPS, schools are often segregated by race/ethnicity, so many schools serve predominantly African American student populations. There is also some segregation by gender in CPS, especially in high schools, as students have different high school choices based on academic achievement. Males tend to have lower test scores and grades, so they have more limited access to some high school options. If these schools systematically suspend students more frequently, that could result in disparities in suspension rates.

After Accounting for Differences in Student Backgrounds, Racial and Gender Differences in Suspension Rates are Still Large

Race and gender disparities in suspension rates are partially related to factors such as neighborhood poverty levels, incoming achievement, and prior history of abuse/neglect or disability status. Students who exhibit these risk factors—those who live in poverty, those with low academic performance, and those with substantiated histories of abuse or neglect—are more likely to be African American. Boys are disproportionately represented among students with disabilities. However, even when taking into account these other factors, large differences in suspension rates exist by race and gender. Differences in risk factors—poverty, prior achievement, disability status, and history of abuse/neglect—only explain about a quarter of the gap in suspension rates between African American and white, and these risk factors explain less than 10 percent of the gender gap.[13]

Even students with no disadvantages in terms of poverty, prior achievement, disability, or history of abuse/neglect are sometimes suspended, especially if they are African American or male. **Figure 3** shows suspension rates by race and gender for those students

FIGURE 3

There Are Large Racial/Ethnic and Gender Disparities among Students with Similar Levels of Social and Academic Advantages

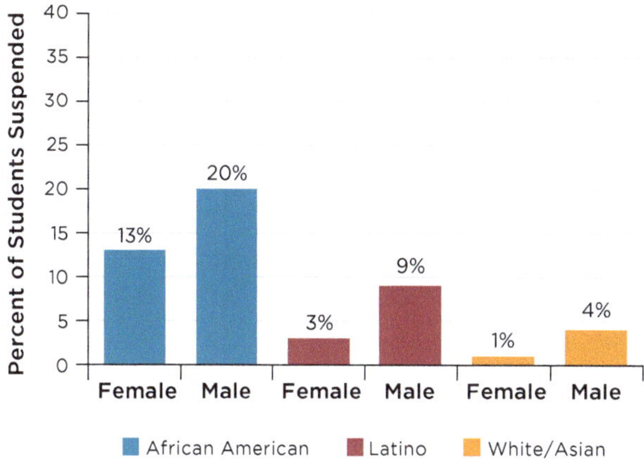

Note: OSS rates for students with above-average incoming achievement, living in neighborhoods with below-average poverty levels, with no history of substantiated abuse or neglect, and no identified learning disabilities. There are over 1,200 students in each subgroup.

12 There is experimental evidence that teachers, on average, perceive the same misbehavior as more troubling and in need of discipline if they believe it was done by an African American student rather than by a white student (Okonofua & Eberhardt, 2015), that African American behaviors are seen as more aggressive than white (Duncan, 1976; Devine, 1989), and that boys' actions are perceived as more aggressive than girls' (Condry & Ross, 1985; de Meijer, 1991).

13 The size of the African American coefficient in linear probability models that control for socio-economic factors is reduced by 25 percent, compared to a model without them, while the gender coefficient is reduced by 8 percent at the middle grade level and 6 percent at the high school level.

who do not exhibit other risk factors for suspension—they live in neighborhoods with below-average poverty levels, have above-average incoming test scores, do not have IEPs, and do not have a reported history of abuse or neglect. African American students with no observable risk factors are still suspended at the highest rates compared to other student subgroups—at 13 percent for females and 20 percent for males in high school. Moreover, among students with no risk factors, suspension rates are still one-and-a-half to four times larger for male students than female students of the same race/ethnicity. Ultimately, while African American students are more likely to exhibit these risk factors, this fact does not primarily explain why African American students are suspended at higher rates than other students.

TABLE 1

African American Males Are More Likely To Be Suspended than Other Students in the Same School

Differences in Suspension Rates Compared to Other Students in the Same School (High School Students, 2013-14)		
Student Group	All High Schools	Diverse Schools (40% of High Schools)
African American Males	7%	12%
Latino Males	1%	0%
White or Asian Males	-1%	0%
African American Females	-1%	2%
Latina Females	-5%	-4%
White or Asian Females	-4%	-3%

Note: Positive values indicate that a student group is suspended more than the average suspension rate in the school, while negative values indicate that a student group is suspended less than the average suspension rate in the school. Diverse schools are those where a single race/ethnicity is no more than 75 percent of the student population in the school. When we limit the sample to diverse schools where we can make comparisons of suspension rates of students of different races/ethnicities, the sample size decreases significantly because many students attend schools that are racially segregated.

African American Boys Are More Likely to be Suspended than Other Students in Their School; Other Within-School Disparities Are Small

Another possible explanation for differences in suspension rates by student race/ethnicity is that within the same school African American students are being suspended more often than other students. We find that there is some evidence this is true. **Table 1** shows the difference in suspension rates between the suspension rates at a school for a specific student group (i.e., African American boys) to the overall suspension rate at a school. Positive values indicate that the subgroup is suspended at higher rates than other students, while negative values mean that students in the subgroup are less likely to be suspended than other students in their school. On average, African American boys are at the highest risk of being suspended compared to other students in their school. Suspension rates for African American boys are 7 percentage points higher in high schools. Generally, within the same school, females of all races/ethnicities are less likely to be suspended than male students.

The within-school differences (shown in the column labeled *"All High Schools"*) are constructed from all schools in the district. However, high schools in Chicago are subject to a high degree of racial segregation—a point we discuss in more detail in Chapter 2. Often African American students attend schools only with other African American students; by definition, there cannot be racial differences in suspension rates in these schools. To understand more about racial discipline disparities within a school, we also compare suspension rates by race and gender in schools where the student bodies are racially diverse. These differences are shown in the columns labeled *"Diverse Schools,"* which include schools in which less than 75 percent of the school population is of the same racial/ethnic background. Forty percent of the high schools in our analysis meet this criterion. Within these racially diverse schools, African American boys are suspended at rates that are, on average, 12 percentage points higher than the overall school suspension rate. African American girls are suspended at a rate that is 2 percentage points higher than the overall suspension rate for their school. Latina, white, and Asian girls are suspended at rates that are 3-4 percentage points lower than typical for students at their schools. Latino, white, and Asian boys are suspended at rates that are about typical for their schools.

No matter the schools included in the sample, African American boys are suspended at higher rates than other student subgroups within the same school. However, these within-school differences in suspension rates are not nearly large enough to explain the racial disparities in suspension rates across the district.

Racial Differences in Suspension Rates Are Largely Driven by Differences Across Schools in Their Overall Use of Exclusionary Practices

While there are racial disparities within schools, these within-school differences do not account for most of the differences in suspension rates by race/ethnicity, so we turn to a third explanation: that disparities are driven by differences in suspension rates across schools. Much of the racial disparities, and some of the gender differences, are due to very large differences in the suspension rates at the schools that students attend. Which school a student attends is a much stronger predictor of whether a student will be suspended than any student characteristic, including race and gender, and all of the other risk factors considered previously in this chapter.[14]

Even if students of all races and both genders were suspended at exactly the same rate as other students in their school, there would be substantial disparities in suspension rates by race. This can be seen in **Figure 4**, which shows the average suspension rates in the schools attended by students of different races/ethnicities and genders. For example, African American male high school students attend schools where the average suspension rate across all students is 26 percent. In other words, it is typical for an African American male high school student to attend a school where a quarter of the students are suspended in a year. In contrast, the average suspension rate at the schools attended by Latino male high school students is 12 percent, and by white and Asian male high school students is 7 percent. Girls also attend schools with slightly lower suspension rates, on average, than boys with the same race/ethnicity.

FIGURE 4

Racial Disparities in Suspension Rates Are Driven by Differences in School Suspension Rates

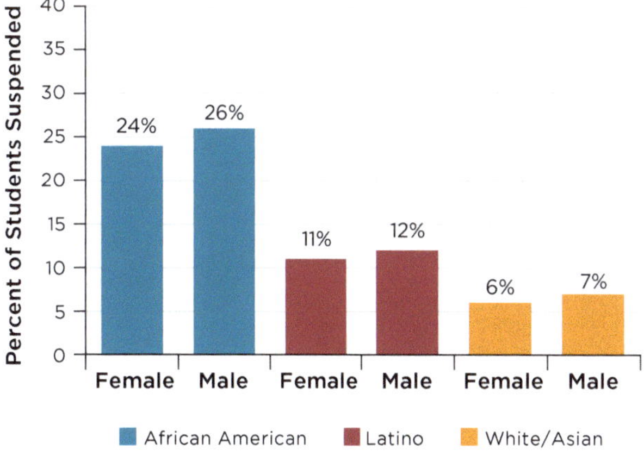

Note: Each student was assigned the suspension rate of the school he/she attends, and then the school suspension rates were averaged across all students in each subgroup (e.g., African American males in high school).

The stark differences in suspension rates across schools suggest a need for a better understanding of which schools have high suspension rates, and how schools differ in their use of exclusionary disciplinary practices, in general. Given that differences across schools explain the largest share of the racial disparities in suspension rates, we now turn to examine differences in the use of exclusionary practices across schools. The next chapter shows the tremendous amount of variation across schools in the use of exclusionary disciplinary practices. The chapter goes beyond out-of-school suspensions to include information on schools' use of other practices that exclude students from instruction (in-school suspensions and arrests). In addition to examining school administrative data on exclusionary discipline practices, the chapter also provides perspectives from school administrators and teachers who were interviewed about the discipline practices in their schools.

14 Student demographics and school effects are strongly related because of the degree of racial segregation in the city's schools. However, the school a student attends explains much more of the variation in suspensions than students' background characteristics alone. Statistical models (linear probability models) that predict suspensions based only on demographic characteristics produce an adjusted R-squared of 0.083. Adding variables for poverty, prior achievement, prior history of abuse/neglect, and special education status increases the adjusted R-squared to 0.093. School fixed effects on their own produce an adjusted R-squared of 0.142. Together, all background characteristics and school characteristics produce an adjusted R-squared of 0.162. Thus, background characteristics only explain an additional 2 percent of variance beyond school effects, while school effects explain an additional 7 percent of variance beyond background characteristics. While school effects do not explain most of the variance in suspension rates, they do explain most of the differences in suspension rates by race/ethnicity.

CHAPTER 2

How Do Schools Differ in Their Use of Exclusionary Discipline Practices?

This chapter changes the focus of the report from subgroups of students to showing differences in suspension rates across schools. As the district continues to encourage schools to reduce the use of suspensions and other exclusionary discipline practices (i.e., disciplinary actions that exclude students from the learning environment), it is necessary to understand the range of school practices around suspension usage to pinpoint which types of schools are relying on suspensions as a primary strategy for correcting student behavior and most need support in this area. This chapter highlights vast differences across CPS schools in their use of exclusionary practices, and shows that many schools use suspensions and arrests at low rates while others use them extensively. It also shows how use of out-of-school suspensions in a school is related to the use of in-school suspensions and police involvement. The chapter ends by showing the stark differences in the student populations served by schools with low rates of exclusionary practices compared to schools that use exclusionary practices at high rates, especially at the high school level.

There Are Large Differences across CPS High Schools in the Use of Exclusionary Discipline Practices

While suspension rates in the district are generally high—16 percent of CPS high school students received an OSS in 2013-14—schools vary widely in the extent to which students are assigned out-of-school and in-school suspensions. The overall suspension and arrest rates mask the considerable variation that exists across schools in their use of exclusionary discipline practices. **Figure 5** shows the OSS, ISS, and arrest rates for each school in the district that serves students in grades 9-12.

A number of high schools have fairly low suspension rates. At about one-third of the high schools (31 percent), fewer than 1 in 10 students received an OSS during the 2013-14 school year. On the other end of the spectrum, almost a quarter (23 percent) of high schools assigned 1-in-3 students an OSS. There are also a few high schools that suspend half or more of their students (8 percent of high schools), making students who attend these schools at extremely high risk of being assigned an OSS. Many high schools also did not use in-school suspensions. Fifteen percent of high schools did not assign any in-school suspensions at all, and many others assigned very few. At a handful of high schools (N=8), over half of the students received an ISS during the 2013-14 school year.

Unlike suspensions, arrests are rare occurrences. At a small number of high schools, however, arrests are fairly common; four high schools had arrest rates higher than 5 percent, or 1-in-20 students arrested at school in 2013-14. In interviews with school administrators, we learned that schools have different approaches when it comes to police contact, ranging from non-stop communication, to police contact at least once a day, to no contact during the entire previous year. Most often, the schools where administrators said they contacted police at least daily were the schools that had police officers located on-site. At these schools, at least one Chicago police officer has dedicated space and the officer is often considered an integral part of the school staff. An administrator at a school with on-site police said, *"I have a conversation with them every day...keep them in the loop of what's happening...and we continue communicating all day long."* Schools on the other side of the spectrum report minimizing police contact because they *"try to keep everything as much in-house as [possible],"* or they noted that their schools do not have severe discipline problems. One principal said, *"We take care of the little things and, knock on wood, the big things have really not happened."*

How to Read Figure 5

This chapter shows that schools vary widely in their usage of exclusionary practices. Figure 5 is structured to show this variation. The three panels show variation in different types of exclusionary discipline practices—out-of-school suspensions, in-school suspensions, and arrests. Each of the vertical bars represents a school, and the height of the bar denotes the percent of students who are subject to a particular exclusionary discipline practice (e.g., an OSS). The vertical bars are sorted from schools that use the exclusionary practice at the lowest rates on the left, to the highest-use schools on the right. Figure 20 also follows this structure for schools that serve middle grades.

FIGURE 5

High Schools Vary Widely in Their Use of Suspensions and Arrests

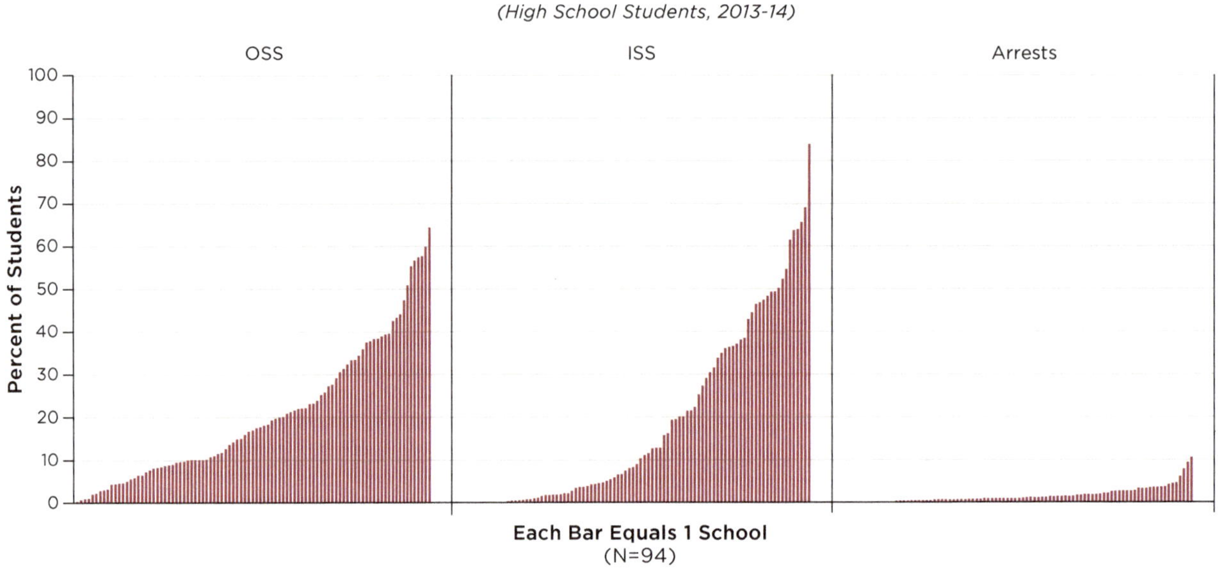

Note: The height of each bar represents the rate at which a specific exclusionary discipline practice is used at an individual school. The numerator is the number of students at a school subject to the exclusionary discipline practice (e.g., the number of students at a school who are assigned an OSS), and the denominator is the total student enrollment at that school.

Schools That Use OSS at High Rates Also Tend to Use Other Exclusionary Practices at High Rates

Prior to conducting this study, we suspected that schools would use different combinations of strategies to address disciplinary issues. For example, some schools might use ISS to a great extent, but not OSS or arrests. However, we found that this was not the case—schools that use ISS extensively tend to be the same schools that use OSS at high rates, and they tend to have the highest rates of police involvement. They also generally give longer suspensions than other schools. It is not the case that some schools heavily use one form of exclusionary discipline, but use another strategy less often. Therefore, when looking at which types of schools use exclusionary discipline practices more than others, it is not necessary to examine out-of-school suspensions separately from in-school suspensions, long suspensions, or arrests. Instead, we divide schools into groups based on how extensively they use all exclusionary practices.

Schools fell into three categories based on the extent to which they used exclusionary discipline practices: low use of exclusionary discipline practices (low EDP), medium use of exclusionary discipline practices (medium EDP), and high use of exclusionary discipline practices (high EDP); each of these is described below. We will refer to these groups throughout the rest of the report. Details on how we categorized schools are provided in **Appendix D**.

About One-in-Four High Schools Uses Suspensions and Arrests at High Rates

Knowing how many schools, and which schools, rely heavily on exclusionary discipline practices can assist districts in targeting policy efforts and supports to the schools that are struggling most with suspensions and the issues that underlie the need for suspensions. A significant number of schools in the district rarely use

Out-of-School Suspensions: Viewed as a Tactic for Managing Student Behavior in the Short Run, Even if It Does Not Address Underlying Problems

Across the 30 teachers and administrators we interviewed about their use of OSS at both the elementary level (schools serving the middle grades) and high school levels during the 2013-14 school year, a tension emerged as educators considered the use of OSS between the goal of improving student behavior in the long term, and the expediency of removing disruptive students from classrooms and providing an orderly climate for instruction for the rest of the students in the school.

Many of the teachers and administrators expressed concerns about the amount of instructional time that students suspended out of school missed as a result of their exclusion from classrooms. Missing instructional time can put students who were already struggling even further behind. Indeed, some teachers explained, disruptive students' misbehavior was often driven by frustration and/or embarrassment at not understanding what was being taught, or performing poorly on an assignment. When students received an OSS for those incidents, educators felt, they often returned to school even further behind their classmates, thereby creating a vicious cycle of misunderstanding, misbehavior, and missed instruction. One teacher observed,

> *That puts them behind in class work, school work, homework. So, then, when they come back [to school], and they've missed out on [that] instructional time, then they're frustrated because we're on something else [now]...[And] then you're acting up again because you've missed out on something [else] and so...you're frustrated because...you're lost and you don't know where [the class] is at.*

In addition, some teachers and administrators expressed concerns about what students would experience during their time away from school. They wondered whether students would be supervised, or whether the consequence of missing school would feel sufficiently like a punishment. As one teacher put it,

> *How effective [out-of-school suspensions] are, I'm not sure...because, I'm not at home with them. So, you [don't] know [whether] it [is] just a vacation for them, or, you know...some [kind of] intervention being put in place at the home when they are suspended....That's the part that you don't know about. You hope...that if they're being suspended that something is being done [at home], so [that] when they come back, that same behavior doesn't exist again, but how certain [are] you that that's happening? You're not.*

Despite concerns about its effectiveness, missed instructional time, and the possibility of creating and/or fueling such problematic cycles of misunderstanding and misbehavior, there remained a persistent belief in the usefulness of suspending students out of school. While educators expressed reservations about OSS and its overall effectiveness, they remained confident that its use was important and even necessary, both for sending a message about acceptable and unacceptable behavior, and to deter students from acting out on future occasions.

When teachers could not find other effective strategies for managing students' behavior within their classrooms, or when a disruptive student was simply not responsive to the range of other options at their disposal, teachers felt that their only recourse was to remove students from the classroom, particularly out of a sense of responsibility for, and fairness to, the other students in the class who they felt were ready and making an effort to learn. As another teacher explained,

> *[When you're] being disrespectful to each other, calling each other out of [your] names...just being disruptive...and I can't get you back on task, and you constantly want to talk across the room or be loud...I have 29 other kids that are trying to work... you [have to] go...I've done everything that I possibly can to keep you in the class for the day, so now you [have to] go.*

On the whole, while OSS was frequently cited as an immediate means of regaining control of a difficult situation and allowing both adults and students time and space to 'cool off,' most of the educators interviewed felt that students who received an OSS were likely to misbehave again, making OSS at best a partial and often temporary solution. One administrator summed up the dilemma, stating,

> *[Giving an OSS] allows the building to come back under control. Does it change behavior? I can't say. But it does allow the building to get back under control and allow[s] de-escalation between the two parties [to occur].*

In-School Suspensions: Viewed as Potentially Better than OSS, but Also Problematic

The use of ISS has risen from 11 percent of high school students receiving an ISS during the 2008-09 school year to 15 percent of students in 2013-14. This rise in the use of ISS has occurred at the same time that the rate of OSS use has fallen, raising questions about the nature of ISS, the rationale for its increasing use, and its perceived costs and benefits.

Among the teachers and administrators whom we interviewed, attitudes towards ISS were broadly similar to the attitudes towards OSS, with some important exceptions. Like OSS, many educators saw ISS as an important tool for controlling disruptions inside classrooms. In some instances, educators viewed ISS more favorably than OSS because of the greater degree of control it offered over how students spent the time they were excluded from classrooms, particularly for ensuring students' safety. As one teacher explained,

> *...I don't know [much about] the environment that they're being exposed to when they go home...At least our [our school environment] is...the best for them. And I don't know, if [an OSS will] make their situation [at home] better or worse. So I would say...I would say no [I don't think OSS is helpful], just because I would rather [the students] be here, inside the school, not exposed to what's out there.*

In addition to the greater control over the environment students experienced, educators also felt that ISS allowed them to ensure that students continued to do academic work, even when excluded from classrooms. During ISS, teachers and principals explained, students are typically expected to continue working on assignments, relieving at least some of the concern about missed instructional time in some educators' minds.

> *All day...[students] are doing work [in ISS] that they're missing in the classrooms...There's a room, literally, right down the hall [here], where there's an instructor, and [the students] are there the entire day. The kids come in with their work and they have to sit there and work all day, except...when they're given a bathroom break and taken to lunch.*

The 2013-14 Student Code of Conduct provides relatively little guidance about the use of ISS, requiring only that *"the student will attend school but will spend the day away from peers and normally assigned classroom instructional settings while completing assigned instructional tasks"* (p. 9). Perhaps predictably, ISS took a variety of different forms in the different schools where we conducted interviews. In some schools, teachers and administrators described the development of ISS practices that were explicitly aimed at encouraging students to reflect on the transgressions that led to them being given ISS in the first place. One administrator described this particular use of ISS,

> *[ISS is used] to separate the student from [their] peers, to have them reflect on [their] behavior... They have to write a brief essay, responding to the situation and apologizing and [describing] what they will do to correct the behavior for themselves through their thinking...I want them to have practice, goals, strategies...in our school and even in their lives...that's a skill that they can carry with them.*

At the same time, educators recognized that the use of ISS still excludes students from classroom instruction. And when asked directly about its use in their schools, educators remained acutely aware of this limitation. As one teacher explained, *"It's that day's lessons, except that they don't have a teacher to give it to [them], they just [have to] figure it out."* Indeed, he continued,

> *...A lot of times I think [ISS] hurts more than it helps. [Because] then that kid is behind a couple days, and, we won't see as much...academic progress.*

Coupled with newer and tighter restrictions on the use of OSS and the mounting pressure on schools to reduce their reliance on OSS, ISS can appear to be a viable alternative for meeting both the short- and longer-term needs of both teachers and students. Ultimately, however, the core dilemma of whether, when, and to what end to remove disruptive students from classrooms remains.

exclusionary discipline practices. Over a third of high schools are categorized as low EDP schools. However, just over a third are categorized as medium EDP schools, while one-quarter of high schools use exclusionary practices at high rates.

At high EDP high schools, 43 percent of students, on average, receive an OSS during the school year, and nearly half receive an ISS (**see Figure 6**). About 5 percent of students are involved in incidents where police were contacted. About one-third (36 schools) of high schools are medium EDP schools. At these schools, on average, about 20 percent of students receive an OSS and 16 percent of students receive an ISS during the school year. Occasionally, medium EDP high schools involve the police in disciplinary incidents and give long out-of-school suspensions. Another third of high schools (35 schools) use exclusionary discipline practices at low rates. On average, fewer than 1-in-10 students receive an OSS in these low EDP schools. Rarely do they notify the police or give a long OSS to students.

Schools That Rely Heavily on Exclusionary Practices Tend to Serve Highly Vulnerable Student Populations

Chapter 1 showed that African American students tend to go to schools with the highest suspension rates. In this chapter, we look at more than just the racial composition of schools to better understand which schools have high suspension rates. When viewed from the perspective of schools, rather than individual students, it is clear that the degree to which schools use exclusionary practices is strongly related to the student body composition of students they serve. The differences in school characteristics across exclusionary discipline practice groups are especially stark for high schools; Chapter 5 will show how these patterns differ somewhat in schools serving the middle grades.

Table 2 describes the student populations served by schools based on how extensively they use exclusionary practices. The first column of this table describes all of the schools in the district included in the analysis, and

FIGURE 6

At Schools with High Rates of Exclusionary Discipline Practices Nearly One-Half of Students Receive an OSS in a Year

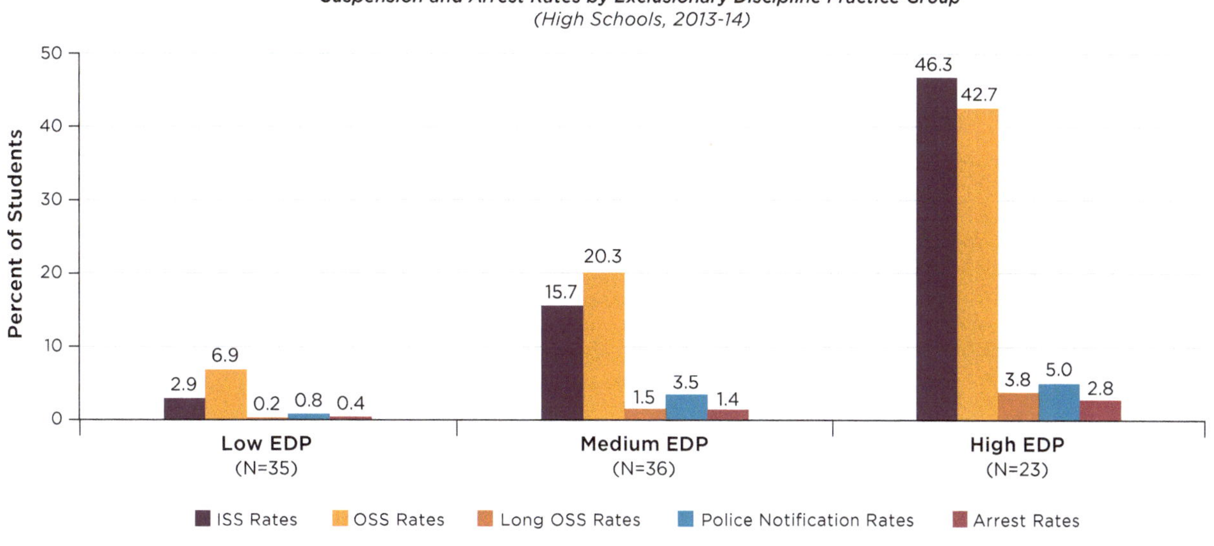

Note: Groups were created using principal component analysis (PCA) including various measures of suspension usage and police contact in the analysis—specifically percent of students at a school who received an ISS, percent of students at a school who received an OSS, percent of students at a school who were involved in an incident that resulted in their arrest, suspensions (ISS and OSS) per capita, whether or not any students at the school were involved in an incident that required police contact (as defined in the CPS student code of conduct), and schools' over or under reliance on police. We used CPS administrative data from the 2012-13 and 2013-14 school years to conduct this analysis. See Appendix D for more information on this methodology.

then the subsequent columns describe each of the school EDP groups. The percentages are to be read as characteristics of the schools in the column. For example, of all 94 schools that serve students in grades 9-12, 27 percent of them have student populations where 1-in-5 students has an identified disability; of the low EDP schools, 6 percent have student populations with this high level of a disability compared to 22 percent of medium EDP schools and 65 percent of high EDP schools.

As we showed in Chapter 1, the school a student attends is a strong predictor of whether or not a student is suspended, and the students who attend schools with the highest suspension rates are often African American students. This finding is supported by evidence presented in **Table 2**. Almost all of the high schools that use exclusionary practices at high rates are predominantly African American, while very few of the low EDP high schools are predominantly African American (91 percent of high-use schools compared to 9 percent of low-use schools). Those that are not predominantly African American serve a combination of African American and Latino students. In contrast, none of the high schools with high suspension rates are predominantly Latino or over 25 percent white or Asian.

High EDP schools serve extremely vulnerable student populations—two-thirds (65 percent) of these schools have a student body where at least 1-in-5 students has an identified disability and *almost all* of these schools have at least 1-in-10 students with a history of reported abuse or neglect. In a classroom of 30 students, in these schools

TABLE 2

Use of Exclusionary Practices in High Schools Is Strongly Related to Characteristics of the Student Body

Characteristics of Schools in Each Exclusionary Discipline Group (High Schools, 2013-14)				
School Characteristics		Exclusionary Discipline Practice Group		
	All Schools (N=94)	Low EDP (N=35)	Medium EDP (N=36)	High EDP (N=23)
Racial/Ethnic Demographics				
Mostly African American	40%	9%	39%	91%
Mostly Latino	19%	23%	28%	0%
Mostly AA & Latino	24%	29%	31%	9%
Racially Diverse (at least 25% white or Asian)	16%	40%	3%	0%
More than 1 in 5 Students With...				
An Identified Disability	27%	6%	22%	65%
More than 1 in 10 Students With...				
History of Abuse/Neglect	31%	0%	22%	91%
Serve Students...				
From the Least Poor Neighborhoods	25%	54%	11%	0%
From the Poorest Neighborhoods	24%	0%	22%	65%
With the Highest Incoming Achievement	27%	54%	14%	0%
With the Lowest Incoming Achievement	24%	0%	14%	78%
Underutilized	61%	29%	67%	100%

Note: Percentages are to be interpreted as the percent of schools in the EDP category that have the characteristic represented by the row. For example, 9 percent of the low EDP schools serve student bodies that are mostly African American. Mostly African American means at least 75 percent of students are African American. Likewise, mostly Latino means that at least 75 percent of students are Latino. Mixed African American/Latino means that the student body is at least 75 percent African American or Latino, but neither group makes up at least 75 percent of the school (i.e., the school is less than 25 percent white or Asian). Racially Diverse means that at least 25 percent of the student body is white or Asian. Schools that serve students from the poorest/most affluent neighborhoods are in the highest/lowest quartile of schools in terms of the average poverty level in students' residential neighborhoods. Schools that serve students with the lowest/highest incoming achievement are in the lowest/highest quartile in terms of their students' average prior test scores.

there are six students with identified disabilities and three students who have a history of abuse or neglect, on average. In fact, 91 percent of the high EDP schools serve a substantial number of students with confirmed histories of being abused or neglected. The vast majority of these schools also serve students who are from the poorest neighborhoods in the city and whose student bodies have the lowest levels of incoming achievement in the district. Taken together, administrators and teachers in these buildings work with students who face substantial challenges and who most likely need considerable support before authentic learning can take place in the classroom. These schools may be difficult places to teach and learn, which is suggested by the fact that all of them are underutilized (according to CPS records on utilization).

In contrast, not one of the low EDP high schools serve student bodies that enter high school from the poorest neighborhoods in the city or with the lowest levels of average incoming achievement. None of the low EDP high schools serves a sizable number of students with histories of having been abused or neglected. Only two of these high schools serve a student body where 1-in-5 students has an identified disability. Thus, high schools with low use of exclusionary practices serve students who have much more advantaged backgrounds than the students at schools that use exclusionary practices extensively.

Another way to visualize the relationship between use of suspensions and arrests is presented in **Figure 7**, which shows the relationship among three factors: 1) the extent to which a school uses exclusionary practices (low, medium, or high EDP); 2) incoming student achievement at the school; and 3) the proportion of the school's student body that is African American (in the left panel) or the average poverty level of the neighborhoods where students live (in the right panel).

The level of segregation in CPS in terms of African American students is immediately apparent in the left panel of this figure. The vast majority of schools are either composed of more than 90 percent African American students or serve fewer than 20 percent African American students in their student body; this is shown in the clustering of schools on the right and left sides of the boxes in **Figure 7**. This segregation is one reason that we see fairly small racial disparities within schools, compared to disparities between them; it is hard to have racial disparities in suspensions within schools when so many schools are racially segregated.

The use of exclusionary discipline practices in high schools is strongly defined by the student body composition of the school. All schools that have high concentrations of students who are struggling academically, are African American, and are from high-poverty neighborhoods use suspensions and arrests at high rates. All low-achieving schools that have predominantly African American student bodies use exclusionary discipline practices at medium or high rates. There are only three predominantly African American high schools that fall in the low EDP category; the students at these schools are nearly average or above average in terms of prior achievement. None of these schools serve low-achieving student bodies.

When looking at school poverty level, the relationship among poverty, achievement, and discipline practices is also dramatic. All but two of the high EDP schools are below average in terms of achievement and above average in terms of poverty (in the bottom right quadrant). Low EDP schools are almost always above average or average in achievement and serving lower-poverty students. One thing to keep in mind when looking at the right panel is that most schools in CPS serve students from high-poverty neighborhoods. Our poverty measure is relative to CPS students, which is a population that is more impoverished than all school-aged children in Chicago, in Illinois, and in the country. Even at the CPS high school that serves the students from the least poor neighborhoods, according to our measure of neighborhood poverty, 70 percent of students qualify for free or reduced-price lunch (FRPL). The most affluent CPS high schools, then, serve more FRPL-qualifying students than there are FRPL-qualifying students in an average school nationwide. In schools that are relatively less poor by CPS standards, where the poverty level is between 0 and 1 standard deviations below the CPS mean, on average 89 percent of students qualify for free or reduced-priced lunch. Nationwide, by contrast, about half of public school students qualify for FRPL.[15]

15 NCES data tables: Table 204.10. Number and percentage of public school students eligible for free or reduced-price lunch, by state: Selected years, 2000-01 through 2012-13. Accessed from https://nces.ed.gov/programs/digest/d14/tables/dt14_204.10.asp?current=yes.

FIGURE 7

Schools Using the Highest Rates of Exclusionary Discipline Practices Primarily Serve Students Who Are Low Achieving, African American, and Live in Poor Neighborhoods

(High Schools, 2013-14)

Low EDP

Average Test Scores

2
1
0
-1
-2

0 10 20 30 40 50 60 70 80 90 100

Low EDP

Average Test Scores

2
1
0
-1
-2

-2 -1 0 1 2

Medium EDP

Average Test Scores

2
1
0
-1
-2

0 10 20 30 40 50 60 70 80 90 100

Medium EDP

Average Test Scores

2
1
0
-1
-2

-2 -1 0 1 2

High EDP

Average Test Scores

2
1
0
-1
-2

0 10 20 30 40 50 60 70 80 90 100

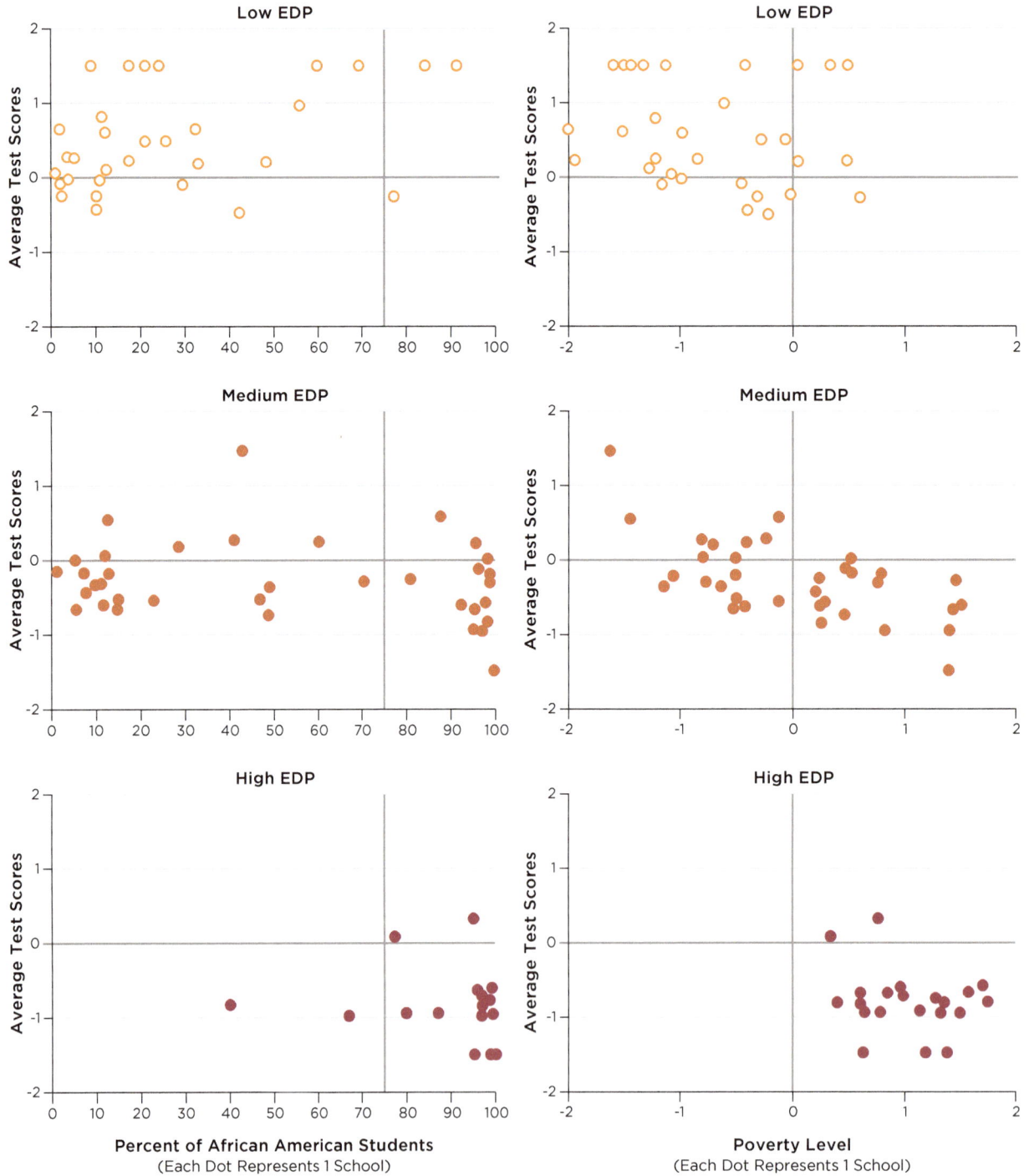

Percent of African American Students

(Each Dot Represents 1 School)

High EDP

Average Test Scores

2
1
0
-1
-2

-2 -1 0 1 2

Poverty Level

(Each Dot Represents 1 School)

Note: Each dot represents a school. The low, medium, and high EDP groups were created using the methodology described in Appendix D. The horizontal line denotes average achievement level. Points above the line are above-average schools in terms of achievement, and the points below the line are below average. The vertical line separates Majority African American schools from other schools. Points to the right of the line serve student bodies that are 75 percent or greater African American.

Note: Each dot represents a school. The low, medium, and high EDP groups were created using the methodology described in Appendix D. The horizontal line denotes average achievement level. Points above the line are above-average schools in terms of achievement, and the points below the line are below average. The vertical line denotes average neighborhood poverty level—relative to CPS students. Points to the right of the line are schools that are above average in terms of poverty (i.e., students live in poorer neighborhoods), and points to the left of the line are schools that are below average in terms of poverty (i.e., students live in less poor neighborhoods).

How to Read Figure 7

Figure 7 shows the relationship of school use of exclusionary practices to both students' incoming achievement and another school characteristic—the proportion of African American students (the left panel) and average neighborhood poverty level of students in the school (the right panel). The figure is divided separately and stacked according to the EDP groups. The top box in each panel is for Low EDP schools, while the bottom box in each panel is for High EDP schools. Each dot represents an individual school. The vertical axis is a measure of incoming student achievement, so schools toward the top of the graph serve students with higher prior test scores, while schools near the bottom serve students that enter the school with lower prior test scores. The horizontal axis represents the percent of African American students in the school (in the left panel), or the average poverty level of students in the school (in the right panel). In the set of figures on the left, to the far right predominantly serve African American students. The horizontal line indicates the average achievement level across all schools, and the vertical line is drawn at 75 percent (our demarcation for predominantly African American schools). The placement of each dot characterizes two things: the average achievement level of the school, and the proportion of African American students the school serves. A dot located in the lower-right quadrant, for example, represents a school that has below average performance and is predominantly African American. For the set of figures on the right side, showing the relationship between test scores and poverty, dots to the right represent schools with higher than average levels of poverty, and dots on the left are schools with lower than average levels of poverty. A dot located in the lower-right quadrant represents a school that has below average performance and serves students who live in neighborhoods that are poorer.

Student incoming achievement matters a lot for discipline issues at the high schools. Regardless of the racial/ethnic composition of the student body or the neighborhoods they live in, there are no low EDP high schools that serve student bodies with extremely low average levels of incoming achievement. High schools serving very low-achieving students almost always rely on exclusionary practices at a high level. Likewise, all low EDP high schools serve students with average or above-average incoming achievement. While there is some overlap in the characteristics of low and medium EDP schools, and between medium and high EDP schools, high schools with low rates of exclusionary practices serve completely different populations of students than high schools with high rates of exclusionary practices.

At the end of the day, almost all low-achieving African American high schools and low-achieving, high-poverty high schools rely heavily on exclusionary practices. It is not students' individual backgrounds that matter as much as the concentration of students with stressful situations—low achievement, high poverty—that makes it likely a school will have high suspension rates. In these schools, all students have an elevated risk of suspension, even students with no prior risk factors. In addition, as the next chapter shows, students at high-suspending schools also experience poorer environments for learning. In Chicago and across the nation, there is a movement to reduce the use of exclusionary practices. The next chapter examines the implications of these policies for school climate and student achievement.

A.P.

CHAPTER 3

How Is Discipline Related to School Climate and Learning?

The use of out-of-school suspensions has been on the decline in CPS, especially at the high school level. The district has emphasized the need to reduce suspensions and to offer other supports to students who display behavioral issues, have conflict with other students, or need to develop social-emotional skills. Given this focus on suspending students less often, it is important to understand how reducing suspensions affects schools and the students who attend them in terms of the climate for learning and student achievement. Chapter 2 showed that the schools with the highest suspension rates tend to serve students who are coming to school the farthest behind, with substantial proportions of their students living in extreme poverty and many who have experienced either abuse or neglect—students who most need a safe and supportive learning environment. These high-suspending schools with vulnerable student populations are also the schools most affected by policies aimed at reducing suspensions. This chapter shows how the use of suspensions is related to the learning climate in the school and student achievement. It begins with simple correlational comparisons among schools serving similar student populations, and then uses policy changes related to the length of suspensions to estimate the effects of shorter suspensions on climate and learning in schools.

Schools with Safer, More Orderly Climates Tend to Use Fewer Exclusionary Discipline Practices

We would expect that schools with low levels of safety, where teachers report many incidents of crime and disorder, would likely have higher suspension rates than other schools, since suspensions are used as responses to misbehavior. At the same time, administrators say that it is necessary to give suspensions as a deterrent to future misbehavior and to ensure that students who are not disruptive feel safe and are given an opportunity to learn unimpeded by behavioral issues. If this is true, we might expect to see that climate is better in schools with higher suspension rates, when comparing schools serving similar student populations—or at least that the relationship between the use of suspensions and school climate is small, since suspensions could be used to prevent misbehavior, as well as to punish misbehavior.

However, schools with high rates of exclusionary discipline practices tend to have much poorer climates for learning than schools that rarely use them. In schools that use exclusionary practices more than other schools, teachers are more likely to report high rates of crime and disorder, and students are more likely to report that they feel unsafe and have poor relationships with their peers. Even when we compare schools serving students from similar backgrounds, those that use exclusionary disciplinary practices to a greater extent have much poorer climates for learning. (**See Appendix E** for estimates of the relationship between school suspension rate and climate, controlling for student body characteristics.)

Teacher survey reports of their perceptions of crime and disorder in the school include physical conflicts among students, robbery or theft, gang activity, disorder in classrooms, disorder in hallways, student disrespect of teachers, and threats of violence toward teachers. (**See Appendix C** for more information on the survey measures used in this report.) The strong relationship between teacher reports of crime and disorder in the school and the extent to which schools rely on exclusionary practices is shown in **Figure 8**. Each bar shows the mean level of crime and disorder across schools in each exclusionary practice category. Low EDP high schools have much lower reports of crime and disorder than medium and high EDP high schools (-0.32 standard deviations below the mean compared to 0.83 and 1.64 standard deviations above the mean, respectively). These differences among EDP school groups are statistically significant, and remain statistically significant and large when we control for the composition of students in the school (as reported in **Appendix E**).

FIGURE 8

In High Schools Where Use of Suspensions and Arrests Is Low, Teachers Report Less Crime and Disorder in the School

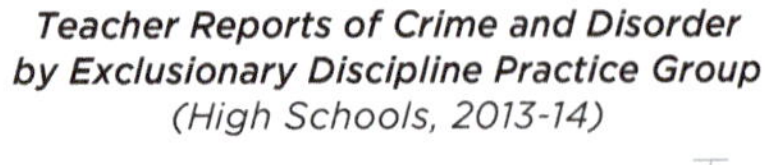

Teacher Reports of Crime and Disorder by Exclusionary Discipline Practice Group (High Schools, 2013-14)

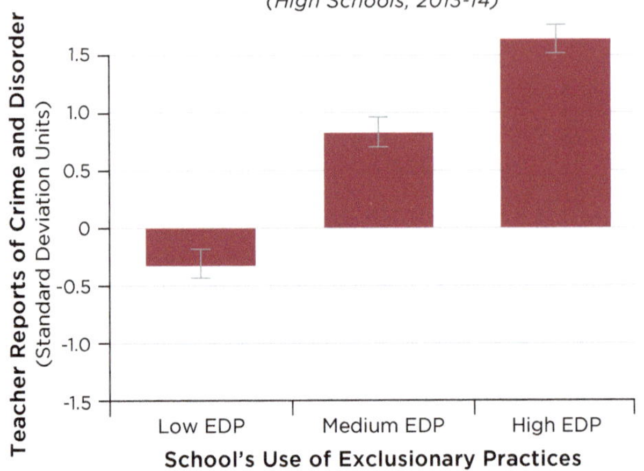

Note: Teacher reports of crime and disorder are captured on the UChicago CCSR/CPS *My Voice, My School* survey. Higher values indicate that teachers report more crime and disorder in their school building. These measures are at the school-level and are standardized across elementary and high schools, allowing for comparisons across elementary and high schools. On average, high schools have higher levels of crime and disorder than elementary schools. Error bars represent uncertainty around the mean, and the true value is somewhere within those bars.

FIGURE 9

In High Schools Where Use of Suspensions and Arrests Is Low, Students Report Having Better Relationships with Their Peers

Student Reports of Peer Relationships by Exclusionary Discipline Practice Group (High Schools, 2013-14)

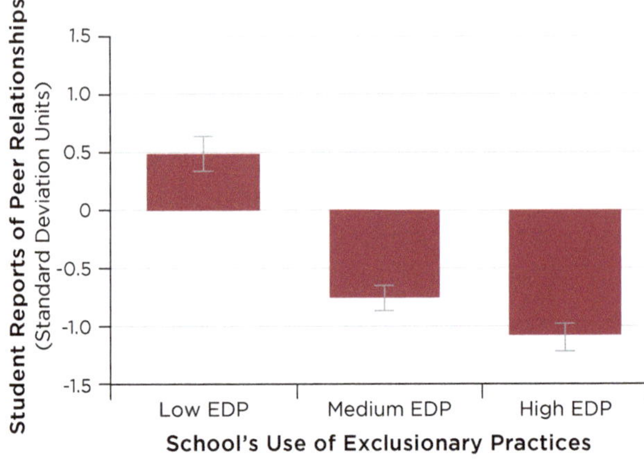

Note: Student reports of quality of peer relationships are captured on the UChicago CCSR/CPS *My Voice, My School* survey. Higher values indicate that students have more positive relationships with peers in their school building. These measures are at the school-level and are standardized across elementary and high schools, allowing for comparisons across elementary and high schools. On average, high schools students have lower reports of peer relationships than middle grade students. Error bars represent uncertainty around the mean, and the true value is somewhere within those bars.

There are similar patterns in student survey reports of relationships with their school peers and their feelings of safety at school. In high EDP schools, students were likely to report feeling less safe than at low and medium EDP schools and to have lower quality relationships with peers (**see Figure 9**). Students reported on the extent to which students at the school like to put each other down, help each other learn, get along well, and treat each other with respect. Students in low EDP high schools respond positively to questions about their peers (0.51 standard deviations above the mean). At the same time, students in medium and high EDP high schools were more negative about their peer relationships (0.75 standard deviations below the mean and 1.09 standard deviations below the mean, respectively). As with teachers' reports of crime and disorder, the relationships between student reports of climate and schools' use of suspensions remain strong even when comparing schools serving similar students.

There is also evidence that school achievement and learning climate tend to be better in schools during the years/semesters in which they give out fewer suspensions. As shown in the first report in this series, students' and teachers' reports of learning climate improved in the same years that there were declines in out-of-school suspensions.[16] This pattern is consistent with findings from a study in Kentucky that showed student learning was higher in semesters where schools assigned fewer suspensions—controlling for the degree of disciplinary problems reported that semester, and examining non-suspended students.[17] It is difficult to disentangle whether schools that are giving out fewer suspensions are responding to improvements in learning climate, or if there are improvements in learning climate in those time points because there are fewer suspensions.[18] However, it is clear that they have a reciprocal relationship with each other—learning climate tends to improve in the same time points when fewer students are suspended.

16 Stevens et al. (2015).

17 Perry & Morris (2014).

18 The Perry and Morris study (2014) controlled for the number of incidents occurring in a school. We do not do that in this study because initial analysis of the data suggests that schools are much more likely to report incidents as occurring when there is a suspension given as a consequence. Records on the number and severity of incidents in a school may not be sufficiently accurate to use in analysis.

Thus, schools with low use of exclusionary practices are very different from schools with medium or high use of exclusionary practices in terms of the climate experienced by students and teachers. Higher suspension rates are associated with lower levels of safety and poorer relationships among peers even when we compare schools serving similar populations of students, or comparing the same schools over time.[19] Students that attend schools with low suspension rates are not only at less risk of suspension, but they also experience a safer, more positive school environment. Prior research in Chicago has shown that school climate is a very strong predictor of student achievement growth.[20] Thus, students at schools with high suspension rates also tend to experience climates that are not conducive to learning.

Appendix E provides more information on the relationship between exclusionary practice usage and school climate measures, as well as relationships between disciplinary practices and school climate for the middle grades.

Reducing Suspension Length: Better Overall Attendance, Stable Test Scores, Worse Climate

The evidence we have presented in this chapter so far is correlational, and the question remains whether or not suspensions cause worse outcomes. It may be possible to improve climate by suspending students less often, or by reducing the length of suspensions that are given. While it is not possible to disentangle the effects of reducing the *number* of suspensions on climate from the effects of changing climate on suspensions, it is possible to examine the effects of the change in the Student Code of Conduct (SCC) requiring *shorter* suspensions. Just prior to the beginning of the 2012-13 school year, CPS made changes to the SCC so that principals had to acquire central office approval if they wanted to suspend students for more than five days (referred to hereafter as long out-of-school suspensions). The district also eliminated mandatory 10-day suspensions and expulsions for the most severe offenses. It is important to highlight that the types of suspensions that the policy limited were suspensions for the worst infractions, those that would have warranted a long suspension, or for students that had multiple infractions for whom other interventions may have been ineffective. Reducing the length of these kinds of suspensions means that the students who were engaged in the worst behavioral infractions were more likely to be in the building, not students who were being suspended for more minor misbehavior. Note that while this particular policy change allows us to look at the effect of reducing these kinds of suspensions in high-use schools, we cannot say causally what the overall effect of using *fewer* suspensions would be, versus reducing the *length* of suspensions.

The frequency with which long suspensions were given—and, correspondingly, the average length of suspensions was shortened—declined in high schools after the implementation of the new SCC. The top panel of **Figure 10** shows high school suspension rates over time in the district. The top line is OSS rates, which have been declining over time. The suspension rates targeted by the policy—those long suspensions over five days—show a marked decrease in the post-policy year. Compared to pre-policy 2011-12 where 3.7 percent of students received a long OSS, in the year after the policy (2012-13) that rate was cut by more than half and 1.6 percent of high school students received a long OSS.

The bottom panel of **Figure 10** shows this information in another way—how many days students were suspended, on average. The top line shows, for students who receive an OSS, the average total days a student was suspended across all suspensions during the year. After the policy, students were missing fewer days of school because of suspension. The bottom line shows the average length of an individual suspension; again the target of the policy was to reduce the length of each individual suspension. After the policy was implemented in 2012-13, the average number of days a student missed due to

19 Steinberg, Allensworth, & Johnson (2011).
20 Sebastian & Allensworth (2012).

FIGURE 10

The Use of Long Suspensions Declined in 2012-13 after Implementing a Policy to Encourage Shorter Suspensions

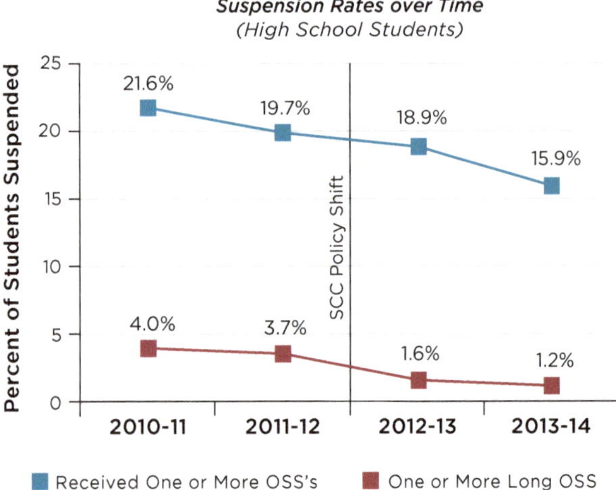

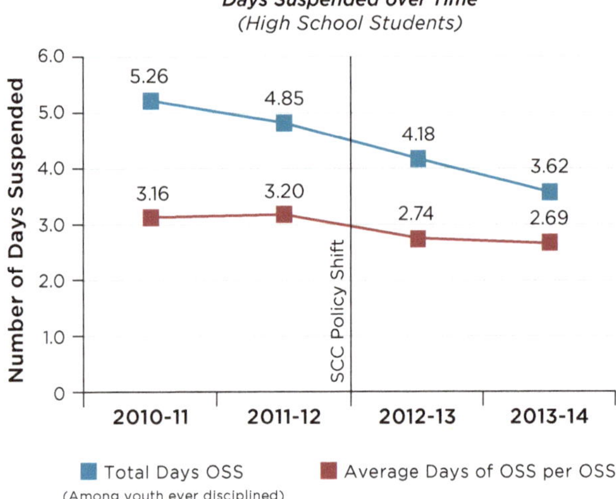

Note: The top panel shows the trend in suspension rates for high school students between 2010-11 and 2013-14. When calculating suspension rates, the numerator is the total number of assigned a suspension (or a suspension longer than five days) in that school year and the denominator is the total student enrollment for that subgroup. The bottom panel shows two indicators related to days suspended (conditional on being suspended)—the average number of days a student was suspended during the year (summed for an individual student across all times the student was suspended) and the average length of a single suspension.

a single OSS was reduced to 2.74 days—down almost a half day from the prior school year (the average length of an OSS in 2011-12 was 3.20 days). We can use this sudden change in the number of days that students were suspended to estimate the effect of reducing the days that students spend in suspension.

Table 3 shows the results of the analysis of the effect of reducing suspensions on student outcomes and school climate. The table shows policy effects for average high schools, and for high schools that used long suspensions extensively before the policy. The latter group of schools would have been most affected by the policy. (**Appendix E** provides information on the sample of students and statistical models.) In schools that relied heavily on long suspensions, student attendance went up by almost four days after the policy change; in the average school, students were in attendance almost two additional days post-policy reform. Some of this is certainly a direct result of the change in suspension practices; if students are suspended for fewer days, then attendance must go up as a consequence. However, these results are estimated for all students in a school—and not just those who received a suspension. This suggests that attendance went up for other reasons as well. Perhaps with shorter suspensions, students feel less isolated from the building and are more likely to attend class. Regardless of the reason for improved attendance, being in school means that students have more opportunities to learn and engage with adults and peers.

Critics of policies aimed at reducing the use of suspensions in favor of more restorative and preventative practices believe that keeping students who misbehave and are disruptive in the classroom in school will detract from the learning of other students. We do not find that learning declined overall. There were no significant changes to reading or math test scores after the policy that mandated shorter suspensions. In the schools that used long suspensions the most prior to the policy change, reading test scores increased by 0.01 standard deviation units, on average, while math test scores increased by 0.02 standard deviation units after the policy was implemented—though these estimates are not statistically different from zero. At best, students may be learning slightly more; at worst, learning remained the same, on average.

While the policy aimed at reducing the length of suspensions seems to have had positive effects on attendance, and test scores remained relatively constant, teacher and student reports of climate actually got worse. Teachers reported the school climate was more disruptive after the policy took effect, and the effects were larger in schools that were using more long suspensions pre-policy. Students also reported having worse relationships with peers after the policy took place than before. These findings are consistent with

TABLE 3

Reducing Suspensions Had Mixed Effects at Schools with High Suspension Rates

Effects of Shortening Suspensions on Student Outcomes (Ninth-Grade Students)		
Outcome	**Average School**	**School with High Rate of Long Suspensions**
Attendance (days)	1.89***	3.75***
Math Achievement Scores (s.d. units)	0.01	0.02
Reading Achievement Scores (s.d. units)	0.00	0.01
Teachers' Reports of Crime & Disorder (s.d. units, **positive is worse)**	0.19***	0.47***
Students' Reports of Peer Relationships (s.d. units, negative is worse)	-0.09***	-0.22***

Note: In 2011-12, the year immediately prior to the policy, the average high school suspended 4 percent of its students for more than five days. On average, high-suspending schools assigned long suspensions to about 10 percent of their students. Test scores are measured on the EPAS. Over this period, CPS changed the test administration calendar. For the 2010-11 cohort, we use the PLAN (given at the beginning of tenth grade), and for the other cohorts we use the EXPLORE (given at the end of ninth grade). To account for differences across cohorts, we standardize within cohort. Survey measures are described in more detail in Appendix C. Asterisks denote statistical significance: *** at the 0.01 level, ** at the 0.05 level, and * at the 0.10 level.

the beliefs expressed by teachers and administrators, as described in the inset box in Chapter 2; many felt that because suspensions removed a disruptive student from the classroom they allowed the teacher to be more effective, even if they felt that suspensions did not seem to solve underlying problems. In fact, we do see that students and teachers felt less safe and noted more disruption when schools reduced the use of long suspensions.

While learning climate declined with the decrease in suspension length, these declines in learning climate were not sufficient to result in lower achievement. Attendance improved, and attendance is strongly related to student learning. At the same time, school climate became worse for both students and teachers, and school climate is also associated with student learning. Overall, the net effect on average learning gains was close to zero. Reducing the extent to which schools can use long suspensions to address behavioral issues seems to have both positive and negative effects on learning, leading to complex implications for principals and teachers. It suggests that school staff need better strategies for supporting positive behavior for suspended students after they return. The next chapter examines the degree to which suspensions are accompanied by practices that might help to improve students' subsequent behavior, besides just removing them from the classroom with a suspension.

CHAPTER 4

Do Schools Supplement Suspensions with Other Supports?

The focus of this report has been on the use of exclusionary practices, particularly out-of-school suspensions. This chapter looks at whether schools use additional, non-exclusionary strategies to address behavioral issues when students are suspended. Out-of-school suspensions are generally given with the intention of punishing a particular student's misbehavior in order to prevent it from reoccurring, as well as to send a message to all students to prevent similar misbehavior in the future. Yet, as seen in the case study box on out-of-school suspensions in Chapter 2, some school staff believe suspensions are ineffective for improving future behavior, or can even make behavior worse. It is also not clear how students' behavior will improve without some attention to what might have incited the issue in the first place. To this end, there are a number of supplemental practices that administrators, teachers, and other staff in CPS can employ to address these concerns. We broadly characterize these supplemental supports as individualized interventions, restorative justice practices, and conferences with parents (see box entitled ***Definition of Key Terms*** **on p.10** and **Appendix B** for a comprehensive list of supports).

Over the last decade, CPS has substantially expanded its support for non-exclusionary strategies that are designed to help schools manage student behavior without relying on exclusionary practices such as suspensions, arrests, or expulsions. CPS has identified the need for schools across the district to mitigate the effects of violence and trauma, as well as build social and emotional skills, implementing a number of high-profile programs designed to address these issues. For example, a partnership with the Collaborative for Academic, Social, and Emotional Learning (CASEL) was developed during this time, and many programs were put into place at various schools, including Conversation, Help, Activity, Movement, Participation, Success (CHAMPS), Dignity in Schools (DSC), and Becoming a Man (BAM). Moreover, the SCC now includes language that endorses the use of restorative practices for some kinds of behavioral infractions. In the fall of 2013, CPS made further changes that reflected a focus on alternative strategies to discipline, providing the Multi-Tiered System of Supports (MTSS) framework as a guide for using the various alternative discipline approaches and instructional supports.[21] The Office of Social and Emotional Learning began providing support to schools as they implemented the MTSS framework.

Thus, CPS has set policy initiatives and practices around creating a safe environment for students, while addressing underlying issues that might lead to school disruptions. However, we have limited data on which schools follow these practices and how schools have changed their practices according to these shifts in policies. Because many schools only record behavioral infractions that result in suspensions, there is unreliable information about what schools do when a behavioral infraction occurs but a suspension is not given. As noted in the Introduction, there are many important questions to investigate regarding non-exclusionary practices that are used as an alternative to suspensions; however, we do not currently have reliable data to examine these questions.

Given these data constraints, this chapter examines the degree to which CPS schools use additional measures (i.e., individualized interventions, restorative justice practices, and conferences with parents) *at the time of an OSS*, rather than assigning the suspension alone. Though we again have no information about the implementation quality of supplemental practices in schools, we have extensive information about the frequency with which schools report the use of various types of

21 MTSS refers to a system designed for schools to use to improve students' academic and social behaviors. To address the needs of struggling students, the system relies on the collection and analysis of student data, and collaboration among school staff, as well as partnerships between schools, outside agencies, and the district.

supplemental practices when a suspension is also assigned. In particular, CPS administrative data (**see box entitled *Data on Supplemental Practices***) allow us to examine differences in rates of supplemental practice usage across schools, the changes in practices over time, and the relationship between the use of supplementary supports and school climate.

About Half of Suspensions Are Given Without Any Additional Supportive Practice

Often when schools give out a suspension, they report no response to a student's infraction other than the suspension itself. In the 2013-14 school year, about half of the suspensions were not accompanied by any supplemental practice, according to administrative records (**see Figure 11**).[22] At the typical school, supplemental practices were used with 48 percent of suspensions in high schools. This means that at the average school, about half of the suspension incidents are not accompanied by a parent conference, or any other supportive practices. At the same time, schools varied widely in the degree to which suspensions were accompanied by supplemental practices. There was one high school that included a supplemental practice with every suspension, another never did, and all others were spread along the continuum.

In nearly all schools, out-of-school suspensions were assigned at least some of the time without a parent conference, restorative practice, or other supplemental support listed as a response in the administrative records. **Table 5** shows the rates of supplemental supports for different types of infractions. Restorative practices may be considered a strategy for responding to interpersonal conflict, though this can be broadly construed. Based on CPS administrative data, there is some evidence that use of restorative practices varies by type of incident. For example, in high school, restorative justice practices are used relatively more frequently for interpersonal conflict violation (i.e., conflicts and threats to safety) than for other types of violations (i.e., defiance and illegal behaviors).

FIGURE 11

The Extent to which Schools Report Supplementing Suspensions with Other Practices and Strategies Varies Widely

School-Level Rates of Supplemental Support Usage
(High Schools, 2013-14)

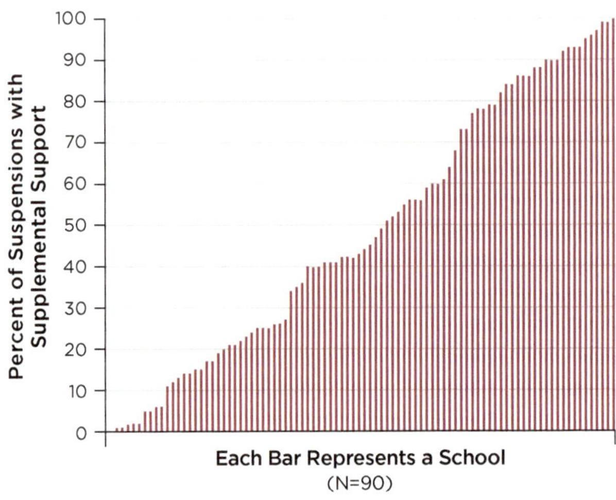

Note: We use CPS administrative data from the 2013-14 school year for schools recording at least 10 suspensions during the school year. There are 90 high schools (including schools that serve students that span the middle and high school grades) that meet this criterion. When calculating support rates, the numerator is the total number of incidents for which a school assigned both an OSS and a supplemental support (see Appendix B) in that school year, and the denominator is the total number of incidents for which an OSS was given in the school.

Individualized interventions are less about responding to particular types of infractions and more about assessing the likelihood that a student would benefit from more focused, personal attention, such as that offered by behavioral contracts or counseling services. CPS specifies that these strategies be used only after other types of practices have failed. The data indeed suggests that these types of practices are used less often than either restorative justice practices or parent conferences regardless of the type of incident (**see Table 5**).

While restorative justice practices and individualized interventions are not necessarily appropriate for all incidents or all students, a conference with a parent when a student is removed from the school building might be considered an appropriate action irrespective of the type of infraction. Parent conferences are the most common response, but they are still paired with suspensions for less than 50 percent

22 The figures and statistics in this chapter are based only on schools that reported at least ten incidents that resulted in suspensions during the 2013-14 school year.

Data on Supplemental Practices: Comparing Administrative Data to Survey Data

CPS administrative misconduct data is the primary source of data on supplemental practices used in this chapter. When a school cites a student for an infraction in the CPS data system, there is an option to select the type of conference that a student attended, as well as any other type of action that was taken. A full list of the types of conference and other actions schools can choose from is included in **Appendix B**.

The 2014 *My Voice, My School* survey of school administrators provides a point of comparison for the administrative misconduct data. In the survey, principals and assistant principals are asked to respond to a number of questions about themselves and their schools.[A] One question asks how often someone from the school met with a family member when a suspension was given to a student. As shown in **Figure A**, in those schools where administrative records show a greater use of parent conference, we also see that administrators at those schools report using parent conferences more frequently but, notably, in most cases administrators report using parent conference more often than the administrative records indicate.

There are many possible reasons why these reports are correlated, but not the same. For example, the wording in the administrative data and the administrator survey are not exactly the same, which could lead to differences in both interpretation and reporting. It could also be that administrators who complete the survey, even if in charge of discipline, are not in charge of recording the incident and accompanying actions in the official records. Likewise, it might be socially desirable to report more family meetings, or alternatively, conferences could occur frequently but they may fail to ever get reported in the administrative data. Regardless of the source of the discrepancies between the two types of data, there is some degree of correlation, and this positive relationship between the two types of data provides some evidence for the validity of the administrative data on supplemental practices that accompany suspensions. However, it is possible that the administrative data is an undercount of what occurs at the school, and we want to acknowledge that possibility. Accuracy of the data is important for understanding what happens in schools and should be a point of emphasis for the district (see Introduction).

FIGURE A

Nearly All High School Administrators Report Regularly Meeting with the Families of Suspended Students

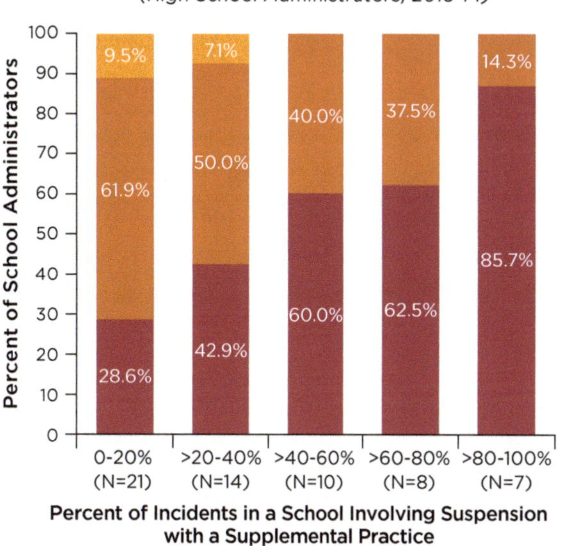

Note: This figure is based on responses to the administrator survey. Response options include Never, Rarely, Usually, Every Suspension. No administrator responded Never. Data is restricted to administrators from schools with ten or more suspensions. Administrators from 60 schools met this criterion. When multiple administrators from the same school responded to the survey, we used the principal's response; if the principal did not respond, we used the assistant principal who indicated that he/she was in charge of discipline; if none of these criteria were met, we selected an assistant principal at random. Schools are grouped along the x-axis based on how often suspensions are paired with supplemental practices according to the administrative data records (number of schools in each group is given in the parentheses). The schools in this figure are restricted to those with at least 10 reported out-of-school suspensions.

A In cases in which more than one administrator per school completed the survey, only one response was used. The principal's response was used if available. If there was no principal, then the assistant principal who noted that he/she is in charge of discipline was selected. If none of all the assistant principals reported being in charge of discipline, an assistant principal was randomly selected.

TABLE 5

Supplemental Supports Are Used More Often When the Incident Involves a Conflict or Threat to Safety and Illegal Behaviors

Supplemental Support Rates by Type of Incident (High Schools, 2013-14)				
Type of Infraction	Type of Supplemental Practice			
	Individualized	Restorative Justice	Parent Conference	Any Supplemental Support
Defiance and Violations of School Rules	3%	16%	28%	40%
Conflict and Threats to Safety	4%	18%	39%	50%
Illegal Behaviors	4%	13%	41%	49%

Note: The percentages in the table are averages of school-level average rates of supplemental support usage by type of infraction. For more information on how infractions are coded, see the first report in this series on discipline in CPS (Stevens et al., 2015). Note that the percentages shown in the Individualized, Restorative Justice, and Parent Conference columns may sum to more than the Any Supplemental Support column. This can occur if multiple supports are provided with a single suspension.

of incidents. A wide variety of factors can contribute to whether school staff meet with a student's parents after the student is suspended. These include factors that staff at some schools have reported feeling are beyond their control. **The box entitled *How Schools Involve Parents when Students Are Suspended*** describes the perspective of two schools on the involvement of families when a student is disciplined for misbehavior.

Reports of Using Supplemental Practices Are Increasing

While the use of supplemental practices may seem low, it represents growth relative to the 2012-13 school year (**see Figure 12**).[23] In high schools, the use of restorative practices nearly doubled from 9 percent of suspension incidents to 16 percent in 2013-14. The percentage of times suspensions were paired with parent conferences increased slightly (3 percentage points), but continued to be paired with only about a third of suspensions in the high schools in 2013-14. Some initiatives for using supplemental supports began a few years prior to 2012-13 in high schools, such as the Culture of Calm. Thus, changes in practice might have occurred in prior years that are not captured when comparing 2012-13 and 2013-14.

FIGURE 12

Rates of Parent Involvement and Restorative Justice Have Increased but Are Still Low

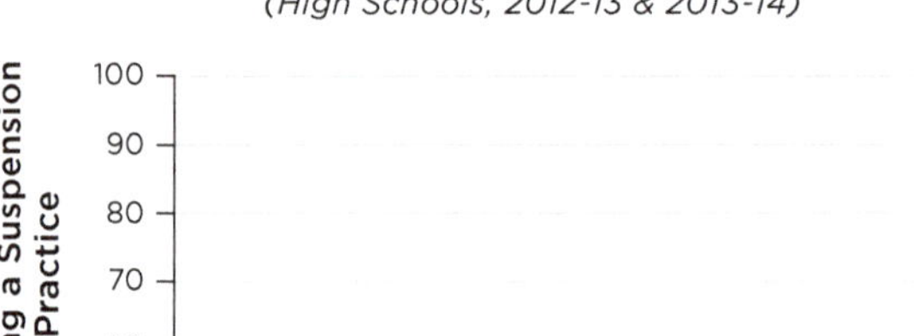
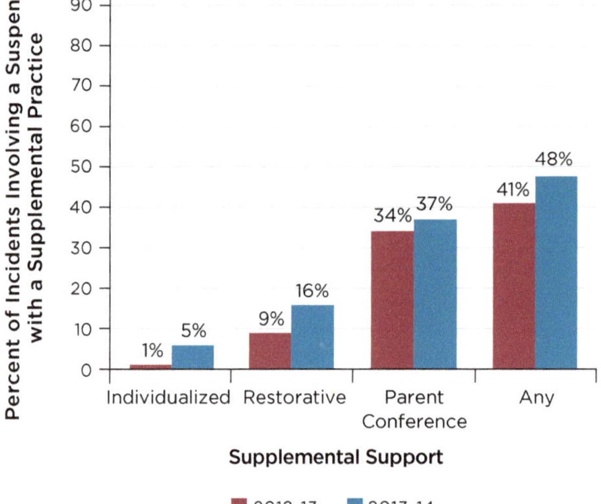

Note: We use CPS administrative data from the 2012-13 and 2013-14 school years for schools recording at least ten suspensions during both years. There are 86 high schools (including schools that serve students that span the middle and high school grades) that meet these criteria. When calculating support rates, the numerator is the total number of incidents for which a school assigned both a suspension and a supplemental support (e.g., restorative justice) in that school year and the denominator is the total number of incidents for which a suspension was given in the school. The Any category includes Individualized, Restorative, Parent Conference, and Other practices. Categories are not mutually exclusive; thus, a single incident that involves a suspension, individualized intervention, parent conference, and restorative practice is included in the numerator of every category. Such an incident is only counted once in the numerator of the Any category.

23 In the 2013-14 school year, there were two fields on the administrative data form that the administrators could populate with a parent conference as a response to an infraction, while in the prior year there was only one field in which to enter a parent conference. This reporting difference might have affected the rate at which parent conferences were reported in 2013-14 compared to 2012-13.

How Schools Involve Parents When Students Are Suspended

The positive involvement of students' parents and families in schools is an aspiration for school administrators. However, building strong, collaborative relationships between home and school can be challenging in many schools and interactions between school staff and students' parents and families surrounding behavior and disciplinary measures, such as suspensions, can be particularly sensitive and difficult. The ways in which administrators and teachers described contact between school and home around discipline varied widely, ranging from relatively rare collaborative efforts to more common formal notifications of consequences.

Virtually all of the educators interviewed for this project described some attempts at communication with parents as a routine part of their approach to discipline. In a few instances, educators described bringing students' parents into a discipline-related decision-making process before consequences were assigned. However, more preventative efforts were not the norm; often parents were simply notified of the consequences that school administrators had determined were appropriate given the behavioral incident that had occurred. This type of interaction was more perfunctory in nature. As one administrator explained,

> *We always make sure that we call parents...to notify [them of] the consequences...We do have to notify them and have that level of communication, to make sure that...the students...adhere[s] to the consequences...but [also]...we want to respect our families as well.*

Many teachers and administrators recognized explicitly that suspending students and removing them from the school placed a greater burden on families, particularly among the families of elementary school-aged children, whose out-of-school care often necessitated rearranging parents' work schedules or making alternative childcare arrangements. For some administrators, this additional burden on families was seen as a reason to assign ISS instead of OSS. On the other hand, some educators described using OSS as an explicit strategy to force parents and families to engage differently with their children's behavioral issues at school, often as a last resort. One teacher described this sort of practice explicitly,

> *For the kids that are...a problem all the time... when they're constantly inconveniencing the staff with their disruptive behavior, we just put that inconvenience on the parent...'Look, as long as this behavior continues, you're going to have to keep coming up here'...We try everything we can to provide that kid with the support [that] they need to be successful, but some kids, really, just have so many issues....they need a more structured environment. And, the only way sometimes to make that happen—and I hate to say this—[is to] inconvenience the parents...*

While educators struggled with how to involve parents, many teachers and administrators noted that parents usually have important insight into their children's behavior. Not only do parents know their own children better than anybody else, they are also aware of the external events and experiences that might influence a child's behavior in the classroom. As one administrator noted,

> *If a student is repeatedly disrespectful then you would call the parent, get the parent involved, get their insight on why the student is being disrespectful, what's going on, what they believe would be the most realistic approach. It could be anything...and the parent can sometimes give you insight, if this [student] is upset [for a reason]—a death in the family, separation of the parents, loss, it can vary, [but once you know], you do what's necessary.*

Despite the challenges educators face in fostering authentic ways for parents to become actively involved in schools, teachers, and administrators generally see parents as important partners in students' educational experience and that is no different when it comes to understanding and addressing behavioral issues.

Supplemental Practices Differ by Racial Composition of the School and Overall Use of Exclusionary Disciplinary Practices

High schools with different racial/ethnic compositions differentially use various types of supplemental practices when assigning suspensions (**see Figure 13**). Predominantly African American schools reported the greatest average rates of restorative practices after an OSS (22 percent of incidents), nearly double the average of schools primarily serving students of other backgrounds. At the same time, a majority of mostly African American schools reported holding parent conferences with

FIGURE 13

Restorative Justice Is Used More Often in Schools Serving Mostly African American Students, though Parent Contact Happens Less Frequently in Those Same Schools

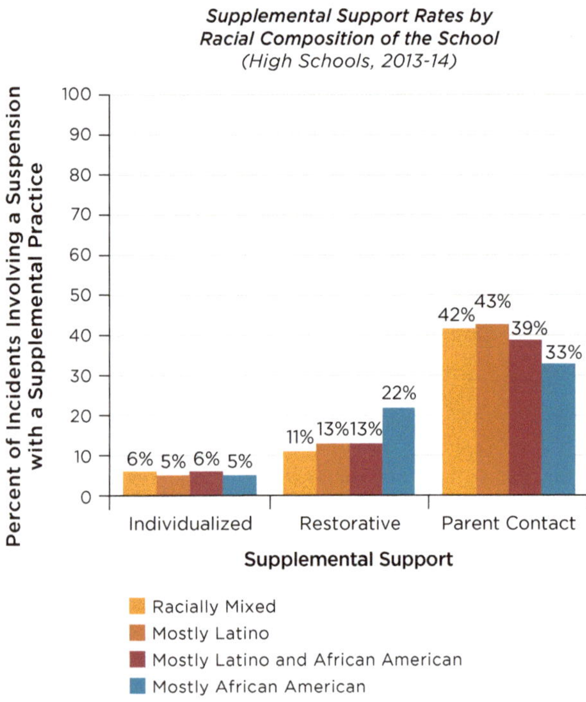

Note: We use CPS administrative data from the 2013-14 school year for schools recording at least ten suspensions. There are 90 high schools (including schools that serve students that span the middle and high school grades) that meet this criterion. A total of four high schools assigned less than ten out-of-school suspensions. When calculating support rates, the numerator is the total number of incidents for which a school assigned both a suspension and a supplemental support (e.g., restorative justice) in that school year, and the denominator is the total number of incidents for which a suspension was given in the school. These rates are calculated for each school and then the school averages are averaged across all schools with a particular student body racial/ethnic composition of the student body. Categories are not mutually exclusive; thus, an incident that involved a suspension, individualized intervention, parent conference, and restorative practice would be included in the numerator of every category. Mostly African American means at least 75 percent of students are African American. Likewise, mostly Latino means that at least 75 percent of students are Latino. Mixed African American/Latino means that the student body is at least 75 percent African American or Latino, but neither group makes up at least 75 percent of the school (i.e., the school is less than 25 percent white or Asian). Racially Mixed means that at least 25 percent of the student body is white or Asian.

somewhat fewer incidents when an OSS was administered than racially mixed, mostly Latino, or mostly African American and Latino schools, with rates of 33 percent, compared to 39-43 percent, respectively. These differences by the school's racial/ethnic composition are tied to larger patterns in the use of supplemental practices based on the extent to which schools use suspensions at all.

On average, schools with low suspension rates tend to report accompanying suspensions with parent conferences more often than schools with high suspension rates. Using the EDP groups described in Chapter 3, **Figure 14** shows that low EDP schools contacted parents 45 percent of the time when a suspension was given, while moderate EDP schools contacted parents for 37 percent of suspension incidents on average, relative to 28 percent of the time in high EDP schools. This does not mean that low EDP schools hold more parent conferences than high EDP schools. In fact, high EDP schools hold a greater number of parent conferences when a suspension is given than low EDP schools on average. But because so many more suspensions are given at high EDP schools than at low ones, a much smaller percentage of suspensions include a conference with parents. When schools give many suspensions, it is likely more difficult to put the time into connecting with parents every time a student is suspended relative to schools where suspensions happen infrequently. Thus, even though high EDP schools contact parents when a suspension is given more times than low EDP schools during a given year, that contact might not lead to increased partnership with parents overall.

Restorative justice practices were least likely to occur in schools with low suspension rates. While medium and high EDP schools used restorative justice practices at about the same rates (18-19 percent), restorative practices were used less in low EDP schools (13 percent). It is possible that this reflects differences in the types of infractions most likely to occur in these schools, and the perceived need to spend school resources on training and staffing for restorative justice programs.

Overall, schools with low and average suspension rates schools are slightly more likely to pair suspensions with supplemental support than schools with high use of exclusionary practices. This is largely driven by differences in the rates at which parent conferences are used. Schools in either the low EDP group or the medium EDP group coupled about half of the suspensions given with a supplemental practice, on average, while high EDP schools used supplemental practices for 42 percent of incidents, on average. At the same time, there is substantial variation in the use of supplemental practices among schools within the same EDP group; some schools in each group almost always accompany suspensions with a supplemental practice, and other schools never do so (**see Figure 15**). That is to say that schools with comparable suspension rates have very different practices around supplementing suspensions with supports. In many high schools, there may be a tension between the potential benefits of using a supplemental practice with a suspension and the amount of resources that a school has to implement them well. The box entitled ***Limited Resources May Constrain Schools' Use of Supplemental Practices*** describes these tensions in schools in the qualitative sample.

Supplemental Practices Are Associated with Better Student Reports of Safety in Schools with Low or Medium Suspension Rates

Even as out-of-school suspensions are getting shorter and being assigned less frequently, many schools still rely heavily on exclusionary practices. As discussed in Chapter 2, school staff that we interviewed often expressed the sentiment that suspensions themselves were not effective for improving subsequent behavior. *In this report, we are not able to say if the use of supplemental practices causes school climate to change, or if the use of supplemental practices leads to schools suspending students less frequently.* These are important questions, but we can only begin to explore the relationship between supplemental practices and school climate.

In low EDP high schools, greater use of supplemental practices is positively correlated with student reports of safety, taking into account differences in climate

FIGURE 14

High Exclusionary Discipline Practice Schools Use Parent Conferences Less than Other Schools

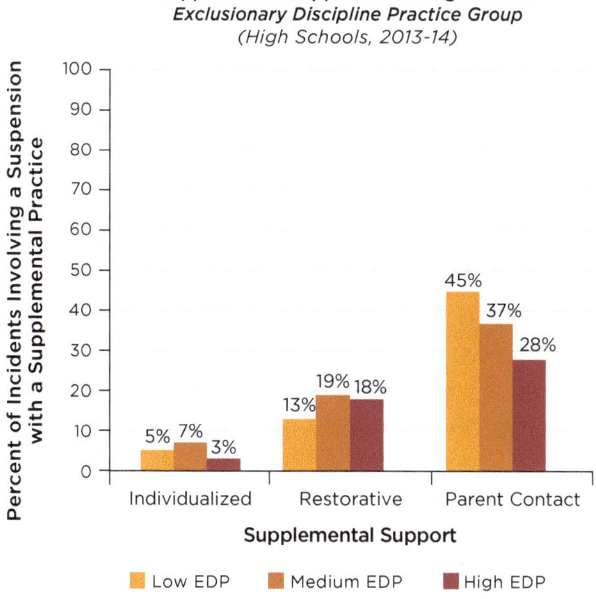

Note: We use CPS administrative data from the 2013-14 school year for schools recording at least ten suspensions. There are 90 high schools (including schools that serve students that span the middle and high school grades) that meet this criterion. A total of four high schools assigned less than 10 out-of-school suspensions. In this figure, there are 31 Low EDP high schools, 36 Medium EDP high schools, and 23 High EDP high schools. When calculating support rates, the numerator is the total number of incidents for which a school assigned both a suspension and a supplemental support (e.g., restorative justice) in that school year and the denominator is the total number of incidents for which a suspension was given in the school. These rates are calculated for each school and then the school averages are averaged across all schools within a particular EDP group.

FIGURE 15

Supplemental Support Rates Vary Widely, Even for Schools that Have Similar Suspension Rates

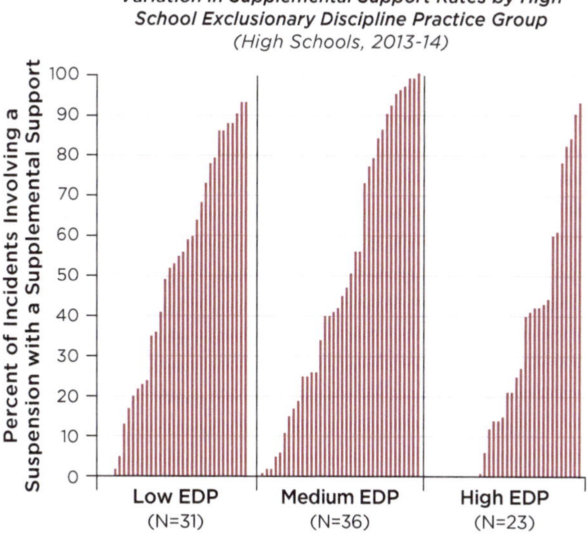

Note: We use CPS administrative data from the 2013-14 school year for schools recording at least ten suspensions. There are 90 high schools (including schools that serve students that span the middle and high school grades) that meet this criterion. A total of four high schools assigned less than 10 out-of-school suspensions. When calculating support rates, the numerator is the total number of incidents for which a school assigned both an OSS and a supplemental support in that school year and the denominator is the total number of incidents for which an OSS was given in the school.

attributable to other school characteristics (**see Table 6**).[24] That is, in schools with low suspension rates, using supplemental support practices more often when a suspension was given was related to a more positive school climate, as reported by students. This relationship appears to be driven by the degree to which suspensions are supplemented by parent conferences, as restorative justice or individualized interventions are used infrequently in low EDP schools. Thus, in schools with low suspension rates, students report feeling safer the more that the school accompanies suspensions with parent conferences.

In medium EDP schools, parent conference use is not significantly related to student or teacher reports of climate. However, rates of restorative practice use are positively related to both student reports of safety and student reports of relationships with their peers. The opposite relationship, however, emerges in schools that heavily relied on exclusionary practices: Using more supplemental supports was related to worse student reports of safety and more problems reported by teachers of crime and disorder in the school. This negative relationship between supplemental practices and school climate is largely attributable to differences in the degree to which schools used restorative justice practices along with a suspension, rather than parent conferences. There is no significant relationship between the use of parent conferences and school climate in high EDP schools.

Limited Resources May Constrain Schools' Use of Supplemental Practices

School administrators describe a number of challenges around supplementing suspensions with additional non-exclusionary supports, given constraints on staffing and professional development opportunities. The sheer scale of time, resources, and coordination necessary to provide students with what they really need is often daunting. Teachers are asked to wear many hats, and policies that seek to reduce suspension use while providing support to students can be taxing. One administrator described how school staff feel overwhelmed by lack of resources,

> *You know...kids are being suspended—but what type of things were [being] done prior to those kids being suspended and by whom? Everybody is stretched, you know—I'm being realistic. Everybody is doing a half of another person's job to try and save these kids. It's tough.*

The conviction that additional resources were needed to meet the demands associated with addressing students' social and emotional needs in the context of misbehavior was consistent across interviews with both elementary and high school teachers and administrators. Educators repeatedly made reference to the challenge of finding the right resources to meet students' needs. Staff were sometimes uncertain about how to access those support staff, who were described as running intensive individualized interventions such as anger management groups or one-on-one therapeutic sessions with particularly troubled students. In the schools we visited, there appeared to be a general sense that the scope of students' needs broadly exceeded the resources available.

CPS administrative data on the number of school staff in the district provides some confirmation to these perceptions. In the 2013-14 school year, there was one counselor for every 255 students in grades 6-12, one social worker for every 550 students, and one psychologist for every 830 students. While not all students need these kinds of services, these caseloads may be daunting, especially in schools that serve large numbers of students living in stressful environments and coming to school with background factors that put them at risk for suspension. In many instances, these support staff are shared across multiple schools, meaning that an individual social worker or psychologist may not be in a particular school building for days at a time, leaving elementary and high school staff with few options for addressing the needs of those students whom they view as most in need of support.

24 The analysis combined two years of data (the 2012-13 and 2013-14 academic years), and controlled for a number of characteristics of schools (e.g., average suspension rates, percent of African American students, and achievement levels in the school) and compared school climates in schools with different uses of supplemental practices with suspensions.

While these findings are informative, they do not allow one to make causal claims about the relationship. School climate could influence the extent to which schools rely on supplemental practices, supplemental practice rates could affect climate, or both. Moreover, a third, unmeasured variable, could account for this relationship. An alternative approach to testing this hypothesis is to examine whether changes in supplemental practices between 2012-13 and 2013-14 were related to changes in school climate over the same period.[25] We found no reliable support for this hypothesis for any category of school; that is, there was no relationship between changes in the use of supplemental practices and changes in school climate. **See Appendix F** for fuller descriptions of these analyses.

Thus, there is some suggestive evidence that accompanying suspensions with supplemental practices—parent contact, restorative practices, or targeted support—may benefit school climate, but only if schools do not have very high rates of exclusionary discipline practices. There is not evidence, however, that increasing the use of supplemental practices necessarily leads to a better climate in any type of school. There are three potential interpretations of these findings:

1. It could be that the district or other organizations specifically provide resources around restorative justice to schools with the worst climates, or that schools that have a greater need to improve their climates are willing to try more restorative practices; thus, it looks as if there is no, or even a negative, relationship when it is just that any benefits are offset by the greater use of these practices in schools with the greatest need.

TABLE 6

In Low-Suspending Schools, Climate and Supplemental Support Usage Are Positively Related; the Opposite Pattern Occurs in High-Suspending Schools

Partial Correlations between Supplemental Support Rates and School Climate by Exclusionary Discipline Practice Group
(High Schools, 2012-13 & 2013-14)

		Survey Measure		
Supplemental Practice	EDP Group	Student Reports of Safety	Teacher Reports of Crime and Disorder (positive is worse)	Student Reports of Peer Relationships
Any Supplemental Practice (including individualized, restorative justice or parent conferences)	Low EDP	.40*	.10	.17
	Medium EDP	.20	-.09	.06
	High EDP	-.48**	.22	-.47*
Restorative Justice Practice	Low EDP	—	—	—
	Medium EDP	.29*	-.10	.39**
	High EDP	-.71**	.45*	-.35
Parent Conference	Low EDP	.37*	-.11	.09
	Medium EDP	.11	-.03	-.10
	High EDP	-.01	-.13	-.29

Note: Eighty six high schools were present in the data and gave more than 10 suspensions in both the 2012-13 and 2013-14 school years. There are 29 Low EDP schools, 35 Medium EDP schools, and 22 High EDP schools. Partial correlations represent the relationship between supplemental practices and student and teacher climate survey measures, after removing common variance shared with other relevant school-level factors, including racial composition, suspension rates, incoming achievement, students' neighborhood poverty, and school enrollment size. All analyses are run separately within EDP group. Analyses of restorative justice practices control for parent conference practices and analyses of parent conference practices control for restorative justice practices. All variables included in the models are standardized and averaged over two years of data (2012-13 and 2013-14). Low EDP schools infrequently use restorative justice practices in the relevant years, resulting in little variation. As such, partial correlation analyses examining the relationship between restorative justice practices and school climate are not reported for this group of schools. Asterisks denote statistical significance: *** at the 0.01 level, ** at the 0.05 level, and * at the 0.10 level.

25 This analysis measured the relationship between the change in supplemental practice use between 2012-13 and 2013-14 and the change in school climate in 2012-13 and 2013-14. The analysis controlled for characteristics of schools in 2013-14, including average suspension rates, percent of African American students, and achievement levels in the school. Neither overall effect nor interaction based on level of exclusionary discipline practice was found.

2. The quality of the supplemental practices likely matters as much as their use, and these practices could be done in ways that either improve or worsen school climate. As discussed, there are barriers to engaging parents in constructive ways and to implementing restorative practices and targeted supports effectively. Without sufficient time, planning, and resources, practices that are intended to be supportive could end up being ineffective; they could lead staff, parents, and students to feel more stress and pressure, rather than more support. In schools that have many disciplinary problems, where both students and school staff are under stress, it may be particularly difficult to effectively implement restorative practices.
3. Restorative practices may work better as substitutes for exclusionary practices than as supplements to them. Due to data constraints, only supplemental practices used with suspensions were analyzed for this study. Many schools use non-exclusionary practices, not only when a suspension is given but also as an alternative to out-of-school suspensions. The effects of using alternative practices instead of exclusionary and non-exclusionary practices simultaneously could be a reason why schools that use fewer exclusionary practices seem to benefit from using supplemental supports. The fact that among high schools with extremely high suspension rates, using supplemental supports more often is actually associated with worse reports of school climate, suggests that schools with high suspension rates are struggling with many issues and need support in successfully implementing supplemental practices both to avoid suspending as many students, and to make it more likely the suspension will actually be followed by improved behavior in the future.

There is a need for more research to distinguish which of these explanations accounts for the patterns observed in school climate and discipline. Knowing which is correct could provide substantial insight into what it takes to reduce disciplinary problems in schools with the most substantial problems. The district has strongly encouraged schools to adopt alternative approaches to suspensions, and many schools have adopted a restorative justice framework. In some schools, though, this framework is being applied while still using exclusionary practices at high rates. Ultimately, these high-suspending schools continue to have substantial problems with order and discipline, even when using restorative practices. It is critical to know what it takes to use these practices effectively in schools that have the greatest needs.

CHAPTER 5

Are Discipline Practices Different in the Middle Grades?

The patterns and relationships that arise in high schools are echoed in middle grades, although suspension rates are much lower and there are many more schools that rarely use exclusionary discipline practices. To the extent that there are differences between middle grades and high school discipline practices, they tend to be in degree, rather than type. For example, there are large discipline disparities across middle grade students, such that African American students, male students, and students with disadvantages are suspended more than other students. However, these disparities are smaller than those in high schools. As seen with high schools, there is wide variation in the use of in-school suspensions, out-of-school suspensions, and arrests across schools serving the middle grades, but all of these practices are used much less in the middle grades than in high schools. In addition, the relationships between the background characteristics of the students that a school serves (i.e., levels of poverty, incoming achievement, race/ethnicity) and the suspension rates of the school are less stark.

FIGURE 16

There Are Large Differences in Suspension Rates by Race/Ethnicity and Gender in the Middle Grades

Out-of-School Suspension Rates by Race/Ethnicity and Gender (Middle Grade Students, 2013-14)

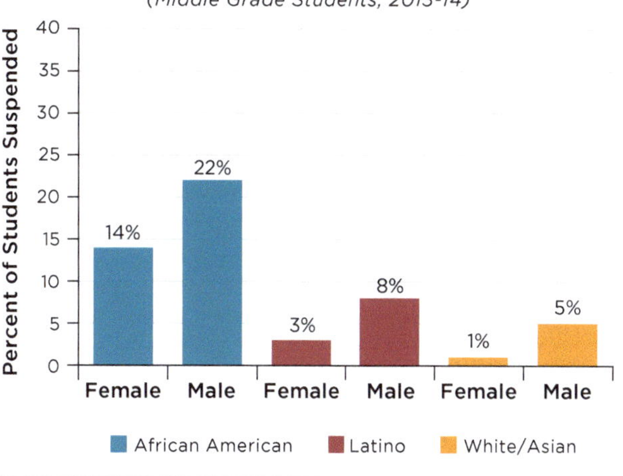

Note: When calculating suspension rates, the numerator is the total number of students in a subgroup (e.g., African American students in high school) assigned a suspension in that school year and the denominator is the total student enrollment for that subgroup. There are 14,196 African American female students; 14,646 African American male students; 17,252 Latina students; 17,867 Latino students; 4,537 white or Asian female students; and 4,896 white or Asian male students.

Discipline Disparities by Race, Gender, and Risk Factors Are Similar to Those in High School

Overall, suspension rates are lower during middle grades years than in high school, and the disparities are somewhat smaller, but the same general patterns hold. During the middle grade years, African American male students are much more likely to receive an OSS or an ISS than male students of other races/ethnicities. OSS rates for African American boys were 22 percent in the 2013-14 school year; in contrast, about 8 percent of Latino boys received an ISS, and 5 percent of white/Asian boys received an OSS (**see Figure 16**). On average, male students were more likely to be suspended than female students, particularly when comparing male and female students of the same racial/ethnic background. Latina and white and Asian female students were suspended relatively infrequently, with OSS rates of 3 percent and 1 percent, respectively. Their male counterparts were suspended at rates that were more than twice as high. African American girls were suspended at rates that were about two-thirds those of African American males (14 percent versus 22 percent). However, as seen in the high school grades, the racial disparities are larger than the gender disparities; African American female students were suspended at higher rates than Latino, white, and Asian students of either gender.

In addition to disparities by racial/ethnic backgrounds, students from vulnerable backgrounds were much more likely to be suspended than students without these risk factors (**see Figure 17**). Seventeen percent of middle grade students living in the poorest neighborhoods received an OSS in 2013-14, compared to 8 percent of students in the least poor neighborhoods. The pattern is exactly the same when comparing suspension rates by incoming achievement. Students

FIGURE 17

Students from More Vulnerable Backgrounds Are Much More Likely To Be Suspended than Other Students in the Middle Grades

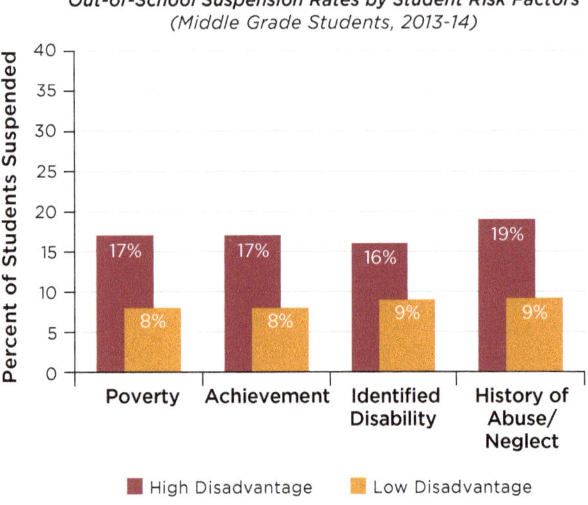

Note: When calculating suspension rates, the numerator is the total number of students in a subgroup (e.g., students who live in high-poverty neighborhoods) assigned at least one suspension in that school year and the denominator is the total student enrollment for that subgroup. High poverty is defined as students living in census block groups in the highest poverty quartile, relative to other students in the district at their grade level. Poverty is measured using U.S. Census data of the percentage of males unemployed and the percentage of families living under poverty in the census block group (which is about one city block in size). The contrast is students in the bottom quartile on the neighborhood poverty measure (i.e., the most affluent neighborhoods). Lowest achievement is similarly the lowest-performing quartile of students in their grade level based on the incoming reading and math test scores (scores from the prior year), contrasted with students in the top quartile on tests. Students with an identified disability had an IEP, excluding 504s, in the 2013-14 school year, contrasted with students without an IEP. Students with a history of abuse/neglect are students who have a substantiated allegation of abuse or neglect in the Child Abuse and Neglect Tracking System (CANTS) of the Illinois Department of Children and Family Services at any point in their life prior to the end of the 2013-14 school year, contrasted to students without a record of having been abused or neglected. The number of middle grade students in the High Disadvantage groups are 18,388 (poverty); 17,966 (achievement); 12,035 (disability); and 3,733 (abuse/neglect).

with an identified disability, or a history of abuse and neglect, had 16 percent and 19 percent OSS rates, respectively, compared with an OSS rate of 9 percent for middle grades students without an identified disability or substantiated history of abuse.

Racial and Ethnic Disparities in Suspension Rates Result From Multiple Sources, but the School a Student Attends in the Middle Grades Matters Most

In Chapter 2 of this report, the potential explanations for the racial/ethnic disparities in high school suspension rates were explored. These explanations included differences between racial/ethnic groups in their background characteristics, such as poverty or prior achievement, differences in the ways students of different racial/ethnic backgrounds are disciplined within the same school, or differences in the types of schools that students of different racial/ethnic backgrounds attend. While no explanation was eliminated—each accounted for some portion of the racial disparities—there was evidence that the school one attends plays the largest role in suspension disparities, such that African American male students attend schools with higher suspension rates than students of other racial/ethnic backgrounds. The pattern of findings is the same for students in middle grades, though the relationships are weaker.

Students of African American backgrounds are more likely to have background disadvantages, including high neighborhood poverty levels, low incoming achievement, and prior history of abuse/neglect or disability status. Moreover, boys are more likely than girls to have an identified disability. Racial, ethnic, and gender differences in these risk factors, however, only explain about a quarter of the gap in suspension rates between African American and white students in the middle grades, and less than 10 percent of the gender gap. African American and male students are at higher risk of suspension than students of other races and compared to girls, even among students with no prior risk factors (**see Figure 18**). In fact, 11 percent of African American male students with no risk factors in the middle grades were suspended in the 2013-14 school year. Thus, background factors are only a partial explanation for racial/ethnic suspension rate disparities.

A second possible explanation for racial/ethnic and gender disparities was that African American and male students are suspended more than other students attending the same schools. In fact, African American male students are suspended more than other student groups at their schools. These students are suspended at rates that are 11 percentage points higher than their school average, among students enrolled in schools with a diverse student body (where no one racial/ethnic group comprises more than 75 percent of students). In contrast, Latino male students and African American female students are suspended at rates that are just 1 percentage point greater than other students in their school, on average, among students attending schools with a racially diverse student body. These within-school differences

FIGURE 18

There Are Modest Racial/Ethnic and Gender Disparities among Middle Grades Students with Similar Levels of Social and Academic Advantages

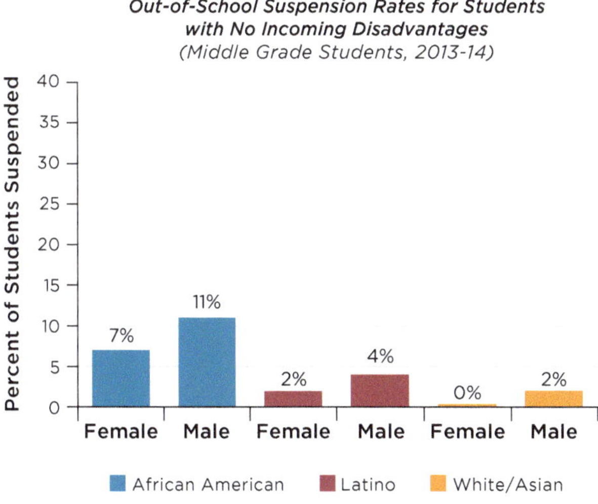

Note: OSS rates for students with above-average incoming achievement, living in neighborhoods with below-average poverty levels, with no history of substantiated abuse or neglect, and no identified learning disabilities. There are over 1,200 students in each subgroup.

FIGURE 19

Racial Disparities in Suspension Rates Are Driven by Differences in School Suspension Rates for African American Middle Grade Students

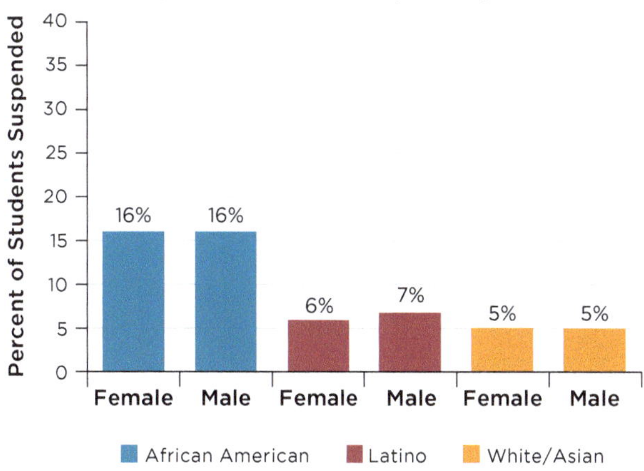

Note: Each student was assigned the suspension rate of the school he/she attends, and then the school suspension rates were averaged across all students in each subgroup (e.g., African American males in middle grade schools).

are important to consider, particularly because they could be the result of biased policies or perceptions about African American male students. At the same time, these differences within schools are not enough to explain the size of the disparities in suspension rates, in particular, for those of different racial/ethnic backgrounds.

Instead, racial disparities appear to be driven by the type of school students of different racial/ethnic backgrounds attend (**see Figure 19**). In fact, the school a student attends is a much better predictor of whether a student will be suspended than any student characteristic, including race and gender, and all of the other risk factors described previously. African American middle grade students attend schools with much higher suspension rates than students of other racial/ethnic backgrounds. This is particularly important, because at schools with very low suspension rates—schools that African American students are somewhat unlikely to attend—few students are suspended, regardless of their race. On the other hand, at schools with very high suspension rates, there are only African American students and about half of the students in the school are suspended each year.

There Are Large Differences across CPS Schools in the use of OSS in the Middle Grades, but Most Have Fairly Low Suspension Rates

Schools vary in the extent to which students are assigned out-of-school and in-school suspensions at the middle grade level. At the average school serving middle grades students, about 1-in-10 students in grades 6-8 (11 percent) received at least one OSS in 2013-14.[26] Average suspension rates can mask the considerable variation that exists across schools in their OSS rates. **Figure 20** shows the OSS rate for each school in the district that serves students in the middle grades.

In-school suspensions are rare at the middle grade level. Over a fifth (23 percent) of middle grade schools gave no ISS, and almost all middle grade schools (91 percent) assigned ISS to fewer than 10 percent of middle grade students. In interviews with administrators at several middle grade schools, they reported not using

26 The district-wide suspension rate for middle grade students in 2013-14 was 10 percent. This rate is lower than the average of school-level rates (11 percent) because small schools suspend at higher rates than average, and all schools get an equal weight in the average of school-level rates.

FIGURE 20

Schools That Serve Middle Grades Vary Widely in Their Use of Suspensions and Arrests

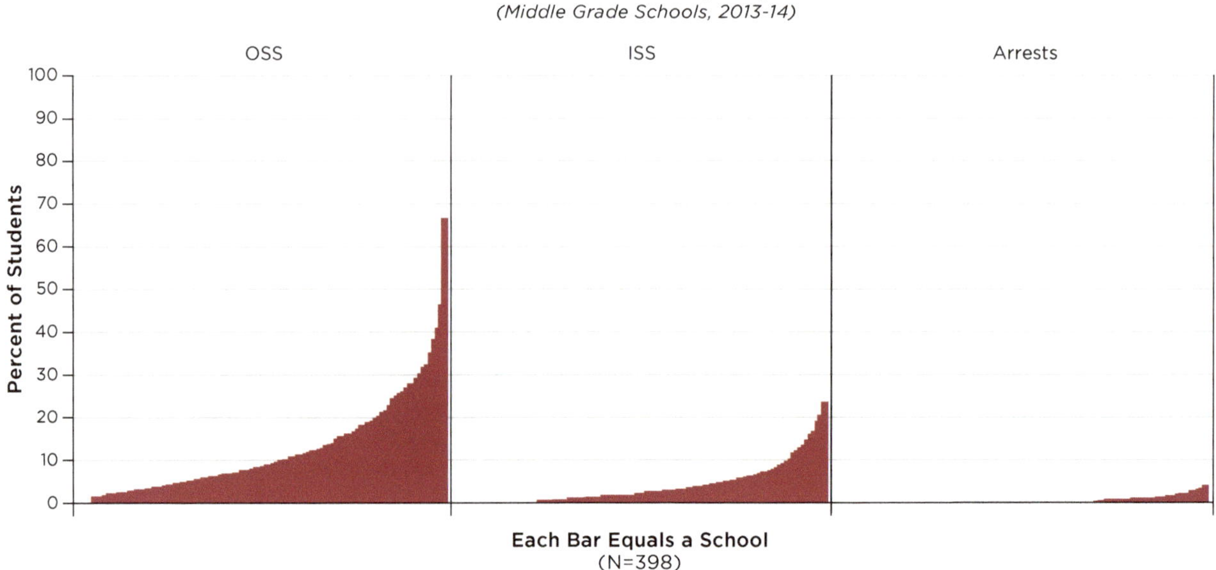

Note: The height of each bar represents the rate at which a specific exclusionary discipline practice is used at an individual school. The numerator is the number of students at a school subject to the exclusionary discipline practice (e.g., the number of students at a school who are assigned an out-of-school suspension) and the denominator is the total student enrollment at that school.

in-school suspensions because of a lack of resources—both in terms of physical space and staffing. As one principal explained, *"We don't have the capacity to have students in in-school suspensions. Who is going to supervise [ISS]? Teachers are doing what they do; I don't want to supervise [ISS], I have stuff to do."* Middle grade schools use ISS less frequently than high schools. But when they do assign ISS, it is, on average, for more days than in high schools, suggesting that ISS is a major intervention in those schools that use it.

Unlike suspensions, police notifications and arrests are rare occurrences in most schools serving middle grade students. At the average school with middle grades, 1 percent of students in grades 6-8 commit an infraction at school that results in the notification of police—which may or may not result in an arrest, while less than 0.5 percent of students are arrested for an incident that occurs at school.[27] That means that most schools serving middle grade students (70 percent) had no incidents that resulted in an arrest in the 2013-14 school year.

As seen with high schools, schools serving the middle grades that use OSS extensively also tend to be the schools that use ISS and have the most police involvement. Therefore, middle grades schools, like high schools, generally fell into three categories based on the overall extent to which they used exclusionary discipline practices: low use of exclusionary discipline practices (low EDP), medium use of exclusionary discipline practices (medium EDP), and high use of exclusionary discipline practices (high EDP). (Details on how we categorized schools are provided in **Appendix D**.) At the middle grade level, the low EDP and medium EDP groups have similar rates of exclusionary practices at both the high school and middle grade level; with low EDP schools suspending about 7 percent of students, on average, and medium EDP schools suspending about 20 percent of student, on average. However, the high EDP high schools use exclusionary practices more extensively than high EDP schools serving the middle grades; while high EDP high schools suspend about 40 percent

27 These statistics only include arrests made at school for an incident occurring at school as reported in CPS administrative data. See the first report in the series (Stevens et al., 2015) for arrest rates among enrolled students for incidents occurring outside of school.

FIGURE 21

On Average at Middle Grade Schools with High Rates of Exclusionary Discipline Practices, Nearly One-Third of Students Receive an OSS in a Year

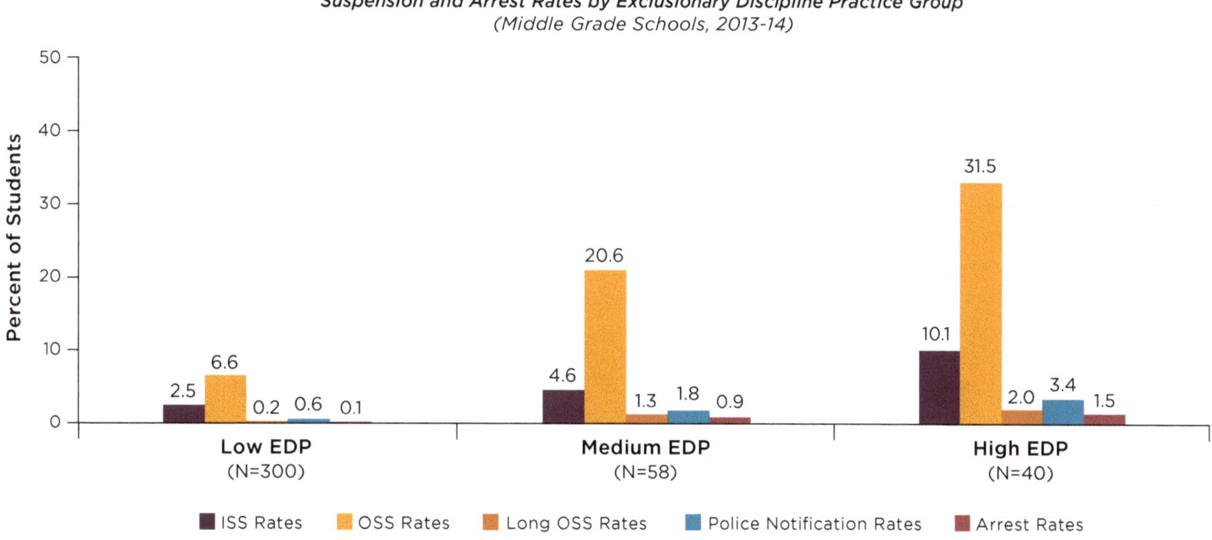

Note: Groups were created using principal component analysis (PCA) including various measures of suspension usage and police contact in the analysis—specifically percent of students at a school who received an ISS, percent of students at a school who received an OSS, percent of students at a school who were involved in an incident that resulted in their arrest, suspensions (ISS and OSS) per capita, whether or not any students at the school were involved in an incident that required police contact (as defined in the CPS student code of conduct), and schools' over or under reliance on police. We used CPS administrative data from the 2012-13 and 2013-14 school years to conduct this analysis. See Appendix D for more information on this methodology.

of students, high EDP schools in the middle grades suspend about 30 percent of students (**see Figure 21**).

Most schools serving middle grades students in the district are low EDP schools, and thus rarely use exclusionary discipline practices. In fact, three-fourths of middle grade schools (300 schools) fall into the low EDP category, where students are at low risk of receiving a suspension and police are almost never involved.

The remaining quarter of schools serving middle grades (98 schools) use exclusionary disciplinary practices fairly often, and are classified as either medium EDP or high EDP schools. In the medium EDP schools, on average, one-fifth of students receive an OSS and 5 percent of students receive an ISS in a year. Arrests at school are rare, but do sometimes occur in these schools. At high EDP schools, about 30 percent of middle grade students receive an OSS and 2 percent of students receive out-of-school suspensions that are longer than five days. Only 10 percent of schools that serve middle grade students are categorized as high EDP schools.

Most Students Experience an Increase in the Use of Exclusionary Discipline Practices When They Move from Eighth to Ninth Grade

When students move from elementary school to ninth grade, the odds of being in a school that uses exclusionary discipline practices extensively increase dramatically. While most schools serving the middle grades have low rates of exclusionary discipline practices, most high schools have either medium or high EDP rates. Furthermore, the suspension rates at high EDP high schools are higher than the suspension rates at high EDP schools serving the middle grades.

Figure 22 provides an illustration of what happens when students move across EDP groups as they transition from eighth to ninth grade.[28] Each bar represents the students who attend a particular type of school in eighth grade—low EDP, medium EDP, and high EDP. The vast majority of eighth-graders attend a low EDP middle grade school, as denoted by the height of the low EDP bar, meaning that most eighth-graders

28 We restrict the sample to students who attended grades 8-9 in CPS and, among those students, to students in both elementary schools and high schools for which we have administrative data on discipline (see Appendix A for more information on the sample). This second limitation generally means that we include only students in non-charter schools in grades 8-9.

FIGURE 22

Students Are Much More Likely To Be Suspended or Arrested in High School than in the Middle Grades

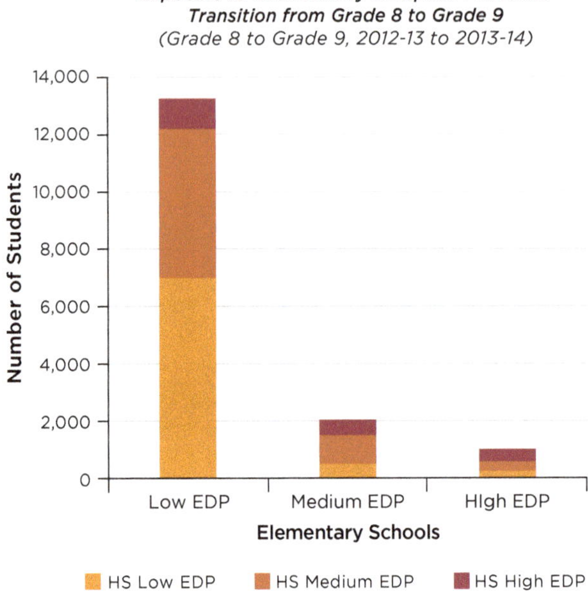

Note: This figure includes information on elementary and high school EDP for a cohort of first-time ninth graders in 2013-14 who were eighth-graders in 2012-13. In order to be included in this analysis, the student must have attended a non-charter, non-alternative CPS school in grades 8-9, making this restriction results in a sample size of 16,226 students.

attend schools where suspension rates are generally low. However, when students move to ninth grade, they are more likely to attend high schools with higher suspension rates than their middle grade school. About half of eighth-graders who attend low EDP middle grade schools also attend low EDP high schools. But the other half go to medium or high EDP high schools; their risk of suspension increases just because of this transition to a high school with higher rates of suspensions and police involvement. Almost all students attend a high school in the same EDP group as the middle grade school or where the EDP group is higher. Of the students in this sample, 52 percent of eighth-graders attend a high school in the same EDP group as their middle grade school. But 42 percent attend a high school with higher rates of EDP than their middle grade school.

Middle School Suspension Rates Are also Related to School Composition, but Less Strongly than High Schools

At the middle grade level, schools with either medium or high EDP rates look different from schools with low EDP rates in terms of their student body composition (**see Table 7**). Both high and medium EDP middle grade schools are much more likely than low EDP schools to serve students with low incoming achievement who are almost all African American. Over two-thirds of high EDP middle grade schools (68 percent) serve students in the lowest quartile of incoming achievement. Many of the medium EDP middle grade schools (55 percent) also serve students with the lowest incoming achievement. Medium and high EDP middle grade schools tend to serve students who need extra supports—about 40 percent have student populations where more than 1-in-5 students has an identified disability, and about 40 percent of these schools serve student populations where more than 1-in-10 students has a history of reported abuse or neglect at home. Two-thirds of middle grade schools with medium or high EDP rates serve students who come from neighborhoods with the highest poverty levels (in the top quartile), and with the lowest levels of prior achievement (in the bottom quartile).

In comparison, low EDP middle grade schools are rarely low achieving. Of the low EDP schools serving the middle grades, only 14 percent serve students from the poorest neighborhoods (where the school-level average poverty levels for students served by the school are in the top quartile of neighborhood poverty), and only 13 percent of these low EDP schools are in the lowest quartile of test scores. Moreover, 29 percent of low EDP middle grade schools are predominantly African American; in fact, many low EDP middle grade schools are racially diverse (24 percent).

An important difference between middle grades and high schools is that many low EDP schools serve students from the most vulnerable backgrounds. While there is a very strong relationship between student characteristics and a school's use of exclusionary practices, not all schools that serve low-achieving African American students from high-poverty neighborhoods use exclusionary practices at high rates. **Figure 23** shows the relationship among three factors: 1) the extent to which a school uses exclusionary practices (low, medium, or high EDP); 2) average incoming student achievement at the school; and 3) either the racial composition (percent African American, in the left panel) or the poverty level of students' neighborhoods.

TABLE 7

Use of Exclusionary Practices in Middle Grade Schools Is Related to Characteristics of the Student Body

Characteristics of Schools in Each Exclusionary Discipline Group *(Middle Grade Schools, 2013-14)*				
School Characteristics		Use of Exclusionary Practices: Schools Serving the Middle Grades		
	All Schools (N=398)	Low EDP (N=300)	Medium EDP (N=58)	High EDP (N=40)
Racial/Ethnic Demographics				
Mostly African American	43%	29%	81%	88%
Mostly Latino	26%	33%	12%	0%
Mostly AA &Latino	12%	14%	7%	10%
Racially Diverse	19%	24%	0%	3%
More than 1 in 5 Students With...				
Identified Disability	31%	28%	41%	38%
More than 1 in 10 Students With...				
History of Abuse/Neglect	18%	11%	41%	40%
Serve Students...				
From the Least Poor Neighborhoods	25%	33%	2%	0%
From the Poorest Neighborhoods	25%	14%	62%	55%
With the Highest Incoming Achievement	25%	33%	2%	0%
With the Lowest Incoming Achievement	25%	13%	55%	68%
Underutilized	47%	37%	74%	83%

Note: Percentages are to be interpreted as the percent of schools in the EDP category that have the characteristic represented by the row. For example, 9 percent of the low EDP schools serve student bodies that are mostly African American. Mostly African American means at least 75 percent of students are African American. Likewise, mostly Latino means that at least 75 percent of students are Latino. Mixed African American/Latino means that the student body is at least 75 percent African American or Latino, but neither group makes up at least 75 percent of the school (i.e., the school is less than 25 percent white or Asian). Racially Diverse means that at least 25 percent of the student body is white or Asian. Schools that serve students from the poorest/most affluent neighborhoods are in the highest/lowest quartile of schools in terms of the average poverty level in students' residential neighborhoods. Schools that serve students with the lowest/highest incoming achievement are in the lowest/highest quartile in terms of their students' average prior test scores.

The middle grade graphs, which contain dots representing hundreds of schools, more starkly display the degree to which there is racial segregation in the district, and the strong relationship between students' neighborhood poverty level and the incoming achievement level of the school. In the left panel, which graphs schools by achievement level and percent African American, the vast majority of schools are either at the far left or the far right of the figures, showing that almost all schools serving the middle grades are either over 90 percent African American or under 20 percent African American. The right panel shows that while there is a great deal of variation in both average student poverty and average incoming student achievement, the two characteristics are strongly related—the vast majority of schools in the three right panel graphs fall into the upper-left or lower-right quadrants. That is to say that there are relatively few middle grade schools in the district that serve both high poverty and high achieving students, or low poverty, low achieving students. Put another way, there is a strong underlying, negative relationship between the level of student poverty and the level of student achievement across schools.

However, unlike the patterns observed in the high schools, there is some variation in the use of exclusionary discipline practices among schools with similar student bodies at the middle grade level. While the vast majority of medium and high EDP middle grades schools serve high poverty students with below-average prior achievement, there are many examples of low EDP

FIGURE 23

At the Middle Grade Level, There Are Schools with Low EDP Rates Serving All Types of Student Bodies

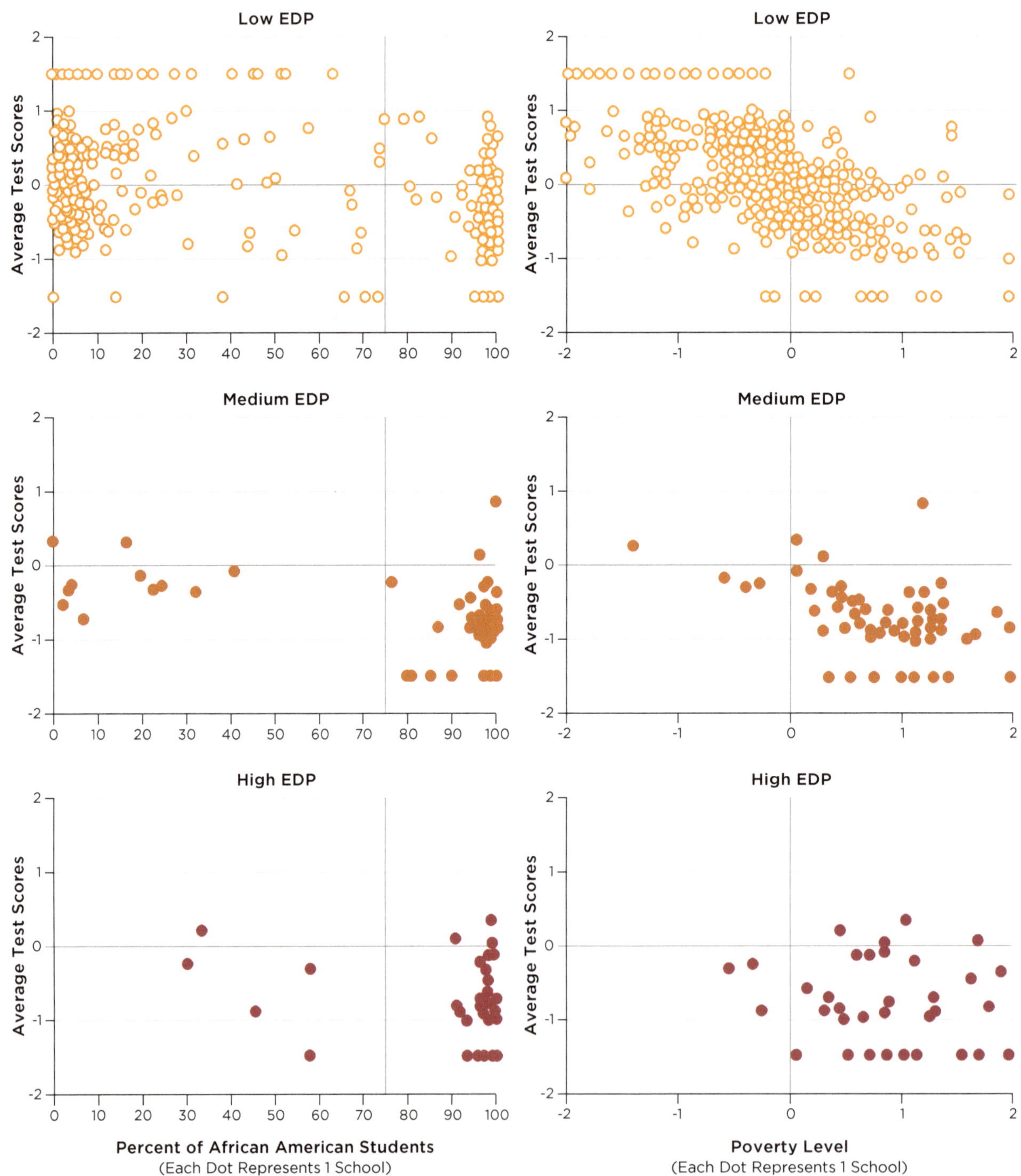

Note: Each dot represents a school. The low, medium, and high EDP groups were created using the methodology described in Appendix D. The horizontal line denotes average achievement level. Points above the line are above-average schools in terms of achievement, and the points below the line are below average. The vertical line separates Mostly African American schools from other schools. Points to the right of the line serve student bodies that are 75 percent or greater African American.

Note: Each dot represents a school. The low, medium, and high EDP groups were created using the methodology described in Appendix D. The horizontal line denotes average achievement level. Points above the line are above-average schools in terms of achievement, and the points below the line are below average. The vertical line denotes average neighborhood poverty level. Points to the right of the line are schools that are above average in terms of poverty (i.e., students live in poorer neighborhoods), and points to the left of the line are schools that are below average in terms of poverty (i.e., students live in less poor neighborhoods).

schools serving low-achieving, high-poverty student populations. There are also some medium and high EDP schools that do not serve low-achieving, high-poverty students. Low EDP schools also serve students with a variety of racial and ethnic backgrounds, even among those that serve students with low average incoming achievement. There are many low EDP schools that serve predominately black or predominately Latino students that are not high-achieving magnet or selective enrollment schools—a pattern not seen at the high school level. In sum, student characteristics do not define the rate at which schools use exclusionary practices in the middle grades to the extent that they do in high schools.

Schools Serving Similar Student Populations that Use Fewer Suspensions Have Better Climates

With high schools, we showed that reducing the length of suspensions may have had a negative impact on climate in schools that used suspensions at very high rates. Because elementary schools so seldom used the long suspensions that were targeted by the policy change, we cannot conduct that same analysis for middle grade students.

On average, students who are the least likely to be suspended, because they attend schools that do not rely on exclusionary discipline practices, are also more likely to experience better school climates. This is true for both elementary and high schools. This finding holds even when comparing schools that have similar student populations. Generally, as a school uses these discipline practices at higher rates, student and teacher reports of climate are worse. The numbers shown in **Table 7** are compared to similar low EDP schools. For example, students at medium EDP schools report feeling 0.25 standard deviations less safe than students at low EDP schools, and students at high EDP schools report feeling 0.42 standard deviations less safe than students at low EDP schools. To compare medium and high EDP schools, subtract the coefficients from each other, so students at high EDP schools report feeling 0.17 standard deviations less safe than students at medium EDP schools.

This pattern generally holds, with the biggest differences in comparing low EDP and high EDP schools, controlling for student characteristics. These differences are large, suggesting that similar schools with higher suspension rates have very different environments. It

TABLE 8

Lower Rates of Exclusionary Discipline Practices Are Associated with Better School Climate

School Climate and Instructional Quality by EDP Use (Middle Grade Schools, 2013-14)		
School Climate Measure	**Medium EDP Compared to Low EDP**	**High EDP Compared to Low EDP**
Learning Climate		
Safety	-0.253**	-0.421***
Crime and disorder (positive is worse)	0.514**	0.600***
Teacher-student trust	-0.117	-0.586***
Student responsibility	-0.176*	-0.175***
Instructional Quality		
Course clarity	-0.185	-0.479***
Academic personalism	-0.075	-0.312*
Academic press	-0.175	-0.528***
Peer relationships	-0.245**	-0.472***
Quality of student discussion	-0.123	-0.700***

Note: The coefficients shown in this table are from a regression of a particular school climate measure on the percent of students who are African American, Latino, special education, and male, as well as the average poverty level of the neighborhoods where students live, incoming achievement, and student enrollment. Omitted group is the low EDP schools, so the coefficients shown are in reference to reported school climate at that group of schools. Survey measures are standardized, so the coefficients represent differences from low EDP schools in standard deviation units. Asterisks denote statistical significance: *** at the 0.01 level, ** at the 0.05 level, and * at the 0.10 level.

also suggests that there is potential to improve climate by finding ways to reduce the reliance on discipline practices that remove students from the school building and isolate students from their peers. While these findings cannot be interpreted causally—that is, we cannot say that suspensions themselves result in worse climates—the evidence suggests that using suspensions less is associated with better climates even at schools serving vulnerable student populations.

In this chapter, we examined how discipline practices in the middle grades are different from those in high schools. We showed that in many ways, discipline practices in middle grades and high schools are similar. That is, racial and gender disparities in discipline outcomes exist; they are driven by a variety of sources, but primarily by which school a student attends. As in high schools, *all* students had the lowest probability of being suspended in schools that relied least on exclusionary practices, were rated as safer, and had better reported climates. In comparison to high schools, however, African American students and students with background vulnerabilities had greater probabilities of being in these low EDP, better climate schools. That is to say that background characteristics are less strongly correlated with the school one attends in the middle grades relative to high school. The smaller magnitude of this effect in the middle grades relative to high schools is promising because it offers an opportunity to investigate lower suspension rates among a broader range of student backgrounds. If one were to only examine high schools, it would appear that race, poverty, and incoming achievement are determinatively intertwined with exclusionary practices. Instead, at the middle grade level, many schools serving large proportions of African American students and students with disadvantaged backgrounds use limited exclusionary practices.

It is worth noting that the differences between middle grades and high school directly impact students' likelihood of being suspended during their ninth- versus their eighth-grade year—even for students with little or no risk of being suspended during the middle grades. There is an exacerbated effect for African American students and students from disadvantaged backgrounds, who are the most likely to attend schools that rely heavily on exclusionary practices in high school. These findings all point to the importance of the transitionary years from middle grades to high school as an area for future inquiry.

CHAPTER 6

Interpretive Summary

Chicago Public Schools is working to reduce the use of suspensions and the disparities in the degree to which they are given. Across the district, the issues that schools face in changing their discipline practices vary considerably, based on the extent to which they use exclusionary discipline practices.

Disparities in suspension rates by students' race/ethnicity, prior achievement, and other characteristics are largely shaped by the uneven distribution of students across different schools in the district. There is substantial racial segregation across schools: Most schools either serve student bodies that are over 90 percent African American, or under 20 percent African American. There is also sorting of students based on neighborhood poverty and incoming achievement levels. Segregation on multiple dimensions is exacerbated at the high school level where there are more options for higher-achieving students, with neighborhood schools in high-poverty areas of the city sometimes seen as a last resort for students who could not get into higher-performing schools. This means that schools across the district face very different challenges. Schools with high concentrations of poor, low-achieving African American students often rely heavily on suspensions and even arrests, while schools that serve more advantaged student populations have fewer behavioral and safety issues to address. Because schools serve such different students, what works in one school to reduce suspensions may not work in another.

CPS is often portrayed as monolith—perceived to be full of schools with extreme disciplinary issues, where students bring weapons to school and engage in drug use. In the first report of this series, we provided evidence that most suspensions were actually for relatively minor infractions like disruptive behavior. These infractions could potentially be addressed through means other than suspensions. In this report, we show that not all schools have extremely high suspension rates; in fact, a third of high schools and three-fourths of schools serving the middle grades rarely use exclusionary discipline practices. Almost all students are at low risk of suspension or arrest in these schools. These schools have student populations that generally begin the school year with higher-than-average academic achievement and may be easier to engage in classroom learning because they do not come to school far behind in terms of prior academic skills. At the same time, most of these schools serve student populations that would be considered *"disadvantaged"* in other school districts, with about 80 percent of their students qualifying for free or reduced-price lunch, on average. They have strong climates despite the fact that they serve more low-income students than typical nationally—they are just relatively more advantaged than schools with moderate to high suspension rates in the district.

A second group of schools have fairly low to moderate rates of exclusionary discipline practices, but there are subgroups of students who are suspended regularly at these schools—most often these are boys—especially African American boys, students with disabilities, and students with low prior academic skills. For these schools with fairly low to moderate suspension rates, reducing suspensions requires examining disparities in the school—discerning why they exist and mobilizing staff to reduce them. There could be issues with staff perceptions of student behavior, so that similar actions are viewed differently based on students' race or gender. Students with weak academic skills or learning disabilities might need more support to meet class expectations. At these schools with low or moderate EDP rates, using restorative approaches, parent conferences, and targeted supports is associated with better school climate, and could help schools to further reduce disciplinary problems. Behavioral issues may be manageable at these schools with small policy changes, especially at medium EDP schools

The most difficult challenges lie with the quarter of high schools and 10 percent of schools serving the middle grades that use exclusionary discipline practices extensively. This group of schools drives the discipline disparities in the district. Almost all of these schools serve predominantly African American students, and African American girls are suspended at high rates in these schools, along with boys. These schools tend to serve students who enter school with very low levels of prior achievement and who live in high-poverty neighborhoods. They serve a substantial proportion of students with confirmed histories of being abused or neglected. Given how many of the students at these schools have histories of being abused or neglected, and live in high poverty, it is likely that many of the students in these schools are also exposed to other elements of high stress—trauma from exposure to violence or tragedy, housing instability, serious health issues in the family—stresses that we cannot measure but that often accompany high poverty. There are structural realities that make it much more difficult to have a safe, orderly environment in schools that are serving large proportions of students living under extreme stress.[29] These schools not only serve students who are often living in extremely difficult circumstances and who are struggling academically, but they are also the schools where it is most difficult to foster good learning climates, where high rates of teacher and administrator turnover make it challenging to establish consistent policies and programs, where instruction may be at lower levels because students may be missing a lot of school due to suspensions or other day-to-day realities, and where teachers have to work hard to help students from falling further behind. With problems this vast, there are no easy solutions.

To address high suspension rates, some schools are providing alternative interventions, such as restorative justice programs. In this study, we see that in schools with very high suspension rates, a greater use of restorative practices to accompany suspensions is actually associated with worse school climate. This may seem counterintuitive, but it could be that schools with the worst climates are simply more willing to engage in alternative strategies—that would lead to a negative association. It is certainly the case that restorative justice programs take considerable staff time and commitment to implement well, and they need to be applied consistently. Teachers and students need to trust that they will be applied fairly. In schools where staff are overwhelmed with high rates of disciplinary problems, it may be particularly difficult to implement these practices effectively. Schools where students report feeling unsafe also tend to have the highest rates of teacher turnover in the district.[30] This churn among teachers, and likely administrators, results in a greater need for continual re-training of staff and greater difficulty maintaining consistent programs. One caveat is that this report does not examine the use of restorative justice in schools as a *replacement* of suspensions, only as a supplement to suspensions. It could be that adding restorative practices on top of suspensions is less effective than using them as a substitute.

A simple strategy to try to reduce the use of exclusionary practices is through district mandates and policies that apply across the board to students in all schools. Yet, policies that limit the use of suspensions can lead to concerns among school staff about whether there will be a negative impact on school climate. In fact, the evidence is mixed about limiting the number of

29 Paulle (2013).

30 Allensworth, Ponisciak, & Mazzeo (2009).

days that students are suspended in schools with high suspension rates through a district mandate. Reducing the length of suspensions, and thereby increasing the presence of students who otherwise may have been serving longer suspensions, led to teachers and students reporting a less safe, more disorderly climate in those schools that had previously given long suspensions. Taken together, these findings suggest that schools with high suspension rates need much better supports to mitigate negative effects on classroom climate when potentially disruptive students are in school longer.

The very strong relationship between the poverty and incoming achievement level of a school and the likelihood that it struggles with disciplinary problems suggests that there are structural factors that underlie the large differences in school climate and the use of exclusionary discipline practices across schools. It further suggests that schools serving the most impoverished students will struggle with disciplinary issues unless they have substantial resources to support students and staff around discipline—such systematic differences would not exist if they were due to idiosyncratic decisions by individuals. Supporting a strong instructional climate in schools serving the most vulnerable, low-achieving students is clearly a challenge. Frequent use of suspensions and arrests does not seem to be effective, given that schools which use these practices frequently have worse climates for instruction than schools that serve similar populations of students that use them less frequently. At the same time, keeping disruptive students in school when there is conflict with other students or a teacher is also not effective for the instructional climate. School suspensions and arrests are concentrated in a subset of schools that serve vulnerable students, leading to questions about whether there are sufficient resources for these schools with high suspension rates, and whether teachers have sufficient training to be effective:

- Do administrators, security guards, deans, and teachers all receive training in strategies for both conflict prevention and conflict resolution, such as PBIS and restorative justice? Is there time for staff to work together to develop and improve their structures for supporting school climate? Schools in Chicago face many competing priorities. School leaders are held accountable to student test score gains, and in the 2013-14 school year, a new accountability framework was implemented, Common Core State Standards were adopted for the first time, and a new teacher evaluation system was fully implemented. Schools serving students with the lowest achievement are under the most pressure to improve in all of these areas, but the amount of time available to provide training to teachers around these priorities is about the same across schools.
- Do teachers in these schools learn about the effects of trauma and stress on students? This could be helpful not only for understanding students' behavior so that it is not taken personally, but also for recognizing signs before problems occur.
- Are teachers trained in de-escalating conflict? As noted in the first report in this series, most suspensions and arrests at school arise because of conflict with teachers or conflict with other students; small problems can easily escalate into big issues when everyone is trying to save face in front of others.
- Do these schools have access to mental health services for their students? As noted in this report, on average across the district, there are hundreds of students for every social worker, counselor, and psychologist in the district. There may be opportunities to partner with hospitals or other agencies to find services for students.
- Are there sufficient support staff for students who need assistance with issues that interfere with their ability to engage in class? Students with low achievement and those who live in substantial poverty often face barriers to engaging successfully in class, from frustration with course expectations, to health or transportation issues preventing regular attendance, to fear of threats from gangs or violence at or on the way to school. Reaching out to students who are poorly engaged in school to find out what barriers they face and help to address them could prevent problems while increasing students' opportunity to learn.

The evidence provided in this report suggests that one-size-fits-all policy changes may not be the most effective way to reduce suspensions. It suggests that there may be a need to find ways to integrate schools with social services and provide wrap-around supports for students who need them the most and the school staff who interact with these students. At the end of the day, due to concerted efforts of district personnel, teachers, and administrators on the ground in schools, and their external partners, suspension and arrest rates have gone down district-wide. Now the biggest gains to be had may be by targeting those schools that are overwhelmed by discipline problems, where nearly half of students are suspended during the school year. Likely accomplishing this feat will require thoughtful targeted policies and supports that address the underlying issues that students and school personnel face.

References

Allensworth, E.M., & Easton, J.Q. (2007).
What matters for staying on track and graduating in Chicago Public Schools. Chicago, IL: University of Chicago Consortium on Chicago School Research.

Allensworth, E., Ponisciak, S., & Mazzeo, C. (2009).
The schools teachers leave: Teacher mobility in Chicago Public Schools. Chicago, IL: University of Chicago Consortium on Chicago School Research.

Allensworth, E.M., Gwynne, J.A., Moore, P., & de la Torre, M. (2014).
Looking forward to high school and college: Middle grade indicators of readiness in Chicago Public Schools. Chicago, IL: University of Chicago Consortium on Chicago School Research.

American Academy of Pediatrics Committee on School Health. (2003).
Out-of-school suspension and expulsion. *Pediatrics, 112*(5), 1206-1209.

American Bar Association. (2001).
Zero tolerance report. Chicago, IL: Author. Retrieved from http://www.americanbar.org/content/dam/aba/directories/policy/2001_my_103b.authcheckdam.pdf

American Psychological Association Zero Tolerance Task Force. (2008).
Are zero tolerance policies effective in the schools? An evidentiary review and recommendations. *The American Psychologist, 63*(9), 852-862.

Balfanz, R., Byrnes, V., & Fox, J. (2015).
Sent home and put off-track: The antecedents, disproportionalities, and consequences of being suspended in the ninth grade. *Journal of Applied Research on Children: Informing Policy for Children at Risk, 5*(2), 13.

Condry, J.C., & Ross, D.F. (1985).
Sex and aggression: The influence of gender label on the perception of aggression in children. *Child Development, 56*(1), 225-233.

De Meijer, M. (1991).
The attribution of aggression and grief to body movements: The effect of sex-stereotypes. *European Journal of Social Psychology, 21*(3), 249-259.

Devine, P.G. (1989).
Stereotypes and prejudice: Their automatic and controlled components. *Journal of Personality and Social Psychology, 56*(1), 5-18.

Duncan, B.L. (1976).
Differential social perception and attribution of inter-group violence: Testing the lower limits of stereotyping of Blacks. *Journal of Personality and Social Psychology, 34*(4), 590-598.

Fabelo, T., Thompson, M.D., Plotkin, M., Carmichael, D., Marchbanks, M.P. III, & Booth, E.A. (2011).
Breaking schools' rules: A statewide study of how school discipline relates to students' success and juvenile justice involvement. New York, NY: Council of State Governments Justice Center.

LaFrance, J.A. (2009).
Examination of the fidelity of school-wide positive behavior support implementation and its relationship to academic and behavioral outcomes in Florida (Doctoral dissertation). Retrieved from ProQuest Dissertations and Theses. (UMI No. 3383666).

Lassen, S.R., Steele, M.M., & Sailor, W. (2006).
The relationship of school-wide positive behavior support to academic achievement in an urban middle school. *Psychology in the Schools, 43*(6), 701-712.

Losen, D.J., & Gillespie, J. (2012).
Opportunities suspended: The disparate impact of disciplinary exclusion from school. Los Angeles, CA: The Civil Rights Project/Proyecto Derechoes Civiles.

Losen, D.J., & Martinez, T.E. (2013).
Out of school and off track: The overuse of suspensions in American middle and high schools. Los Angeles, CA: Civil Rights Project/Proyecto Derechoes Civiles.

Losen, D.J., Hewitt, D., & Toldson, I. (2014).
Eliminating excessive and unfair exclusionary discipline in schools: Policy recommendations for reducing disparities. Bloomington, IN: The Equity Project at Indiana University.

Mader, N., Sartain, L., & Steinberg, M.P. (2015).
When suspensions are shorter: The effects on students and schools (Working Paper). Chicago, IL: University of Chicago Consortium on Chicago School Research.

National Center for Education Statistics. (2013).
Table 204.10. Number and percentage of public school students eligible for free or reduced-price lunch, by state: Selected years, 2000-01 through 2012-13 [Data table]. Retrieved from https://nces.ed.gov/programs/digest/d14/tables/dt14_204.10.asp?current=yes

Chicago Public Schools Office of Social and Emotional Learning. (n.d.).
Strategies. Retrieved from https://sites.google.com/site/cpspositivebehavior/home/about-positive-behavior-supports/strategies

Okonofua, J.A., & Eberhardt, J.L. (2015).
Two strikes race and the disciplining of young students. *Psychological Science, 26*(5), 617-624.

Paulle, B. (2013).
Toxic schools: high-poverty education in New York and Amsterdam. Chicago, IL: University of Chicago Press.

Perry, B.L., & Morris, E.W. (2014).
Suspending progress: Collateral consequences of exclusionary punishment in public schools. *American Sociological Review, 79*(6) 1067–1087.

Sebastian, J., & Allensworth, E. (2012).
The influence of principal leadership on classroom instruction and student learning: A study of mediated pathways to learning. *Educational Administration Quarterly, 48*(4), 626-663.

Steinberg, M.P., Allensworth, E., & Johnson, D.W. (2011).
Student and teacher safety in Chicago Public Schools: The roles of community context and school social organization. Chicago, IL: University of Chicago Consortium on Chicago School Research.

Stevens, W.D., Sartain, L., Allensworth, E.M., & Levenstein, R. (2015).
Discipline practices in Chicago schools: Trends in the use of suspensions and arrests. Chicago, IL: University of Chicago Consortium on Chicago School Research.

Stinchcomb, J.B., Bazemore, G., & Riestenberg, N. (2006).
Beyond zero tolerance: Restoring justice in secondary schools. *Youth Violence and Juvenile Justice, 4*(2), 123-147.

Appendix A

Data Sources

Analysis of School-Level Practices

This study examines discipline practices primarily during the 2013-14 school year. It incorporates administrative data from Chicago Public Schools (CPS) administrative records on suspensions and disciplinary infractions, as well as information about additional interventions that occurred when a student was suspended. We identify students in grades 6-12 (the middle grades and high school years) who are enrolled in regular schools—this does not include students in alternative, special education, or charter schools. Students were considered enrolled if they were enrolled in a CPS school in September and/or May of that school year. This results in 75,982 students in grades 6-8 in 398 elementary schools and 87,259 students in 94 high schools.

Alternative schools—those designed for re-enrollment of dropouts—and schools for severely disabled students are substantially different from other schools in the district in many ways; they are not comparable to regular CPS schools in terms of discipline or instructional measures. Therefore, they are not included in this study. Charter schools do not provide consistent administrative data on misconduct to CPS, and some schools use their own specific discipline codes which are not comparable to district records. Therefore, they cannot be included in the analyses of suspensions.

CPS administrative files contain information on the student infractions that are reported when disciplinary incidents occur. These records tell us why students are getting in trouble, how many students were involved in the incident, and each of the infractions that comprised the incident. While these administrative files tell us which students are getting in trouble, and for what types of infractions, they may not necessarily provide a complete assessment of the problems that are occurring at schools. Schools may not be consistent in the degree to which they are aware of incidents or how they report incidents, or the way that they record incidents if a student does not receive a suspension. For this reason, we focus on suspensions and arrests reported. We look at whether a suspension was an ISS or an OSS, how long the suspensions was, and how many students in a school received a suspension. These data also include supplemental supports that accompanied suspensions, such as parent contact or restorative practices.

Analysis of Suspension-Reduction Policies

The policy analysis presented in Chapter 3 incorporates data from 2010-11 to 2013-14. We use ninth-grade students across those years, resulting in a sample size of 61,518 students. Students in alternative, special education, or charter schools are not included in this analysis.

Specific outcomes that we present include attendance, math and reading test scores, and survey measures of school climate. Attendance is counted as the number of days present (taking into account the number of days enrolled) and comes from CPS administrative data. Test score information also comes from CPS administrative data. We use test scores that capture student performance by the beginning of grade 10. Depending on the year used, the CPS testing policy is different. For the 2010-11 cohort of ninth-graders, we use the PLAN at the beginning of grade 10 as the post-test; for the other cohorts, we use EXPLORE at the end of grade 9 as the post-test. The raw scores are standardized within cohort, which should account for any differences in changes in the testing policy. Survey measures of climate are described in more detail in **Appendix C**.

See Appendix E for more information on the methodology used.

Analysis of Qualitative Interviews

This report draws on extensive qualitative data collected over the 2012-13 and 2013-14 school years. During the first year of fieldwork, in order to capture a range of different disciplinary approaches, we interviewed one administrator from each of 20 different schools—10 high schools and 10 elementary schools serving middle grades—in the late spring and summer of 2013. Schools were selected primarily based on whether they had suspension rates above, at, or below the rate predicted by the prior achievement of the students they served, as well as the levels of crime and poverty in their students' home neighborhoods. Within these three classifications, schools were further stratified by race into schools serving predominantly African American students (more than 65 percent of students) and those that did not. Within these stratified categories, schools were then randomly selected, as shown in **Table A.1**.

TABLE A.1

Sampling Scheme for Interview Schools

Comparison of Actual to Predicted Suspension Rates	Majority African American	Not Majority African American
Higher Suspension Rate than Expected	2 Middle Grade Schools 2 High Schools	2 Middle Grade Schools 2 High Schools
Suspension Rate About as Expected	1 Middle Grade School 1 High School	1 Middle Grade School 1 High School
Lower Suspension Rate than Expected	2 Middle Grade Schools 2 High Schools	2 Middle Grade Schools 2 High Schools

Appendix B

Methods for Analyzing the Effects of Supplemental Practices

Restorative Justice

- Circles
- Mediation
- Peer Conferencing
- Peer Jury
- Peer Jury/Council
- Peer Mediation
- Restorative Conversations
- Restorative Group Conferencing
- Restorative Group Counseling
- Restorative/Peace Circle
- Parent Conference
- Victim Impact Panel
- Victim Offender Conferencing

Individualized Interventions

- Assignment to Counseling Services
- FBA/Behavior Intervention Plan
- Behavioral Contract/Report Card
- Behavioral Contract
- Social Skills Instruction/Tutoring/Mini-Course
- Check In/Check Out
- Community Service
- Community Service/Meaningful Work
- Self-Reflection Sheet

Other

- Referral to Intervention
- Referral to Program
- District Intervention Program Referral

Conferences

- Parent, Administrator, Teacher

Appendix C

Survey Measures

Chapter 3 examines the relationship between a school's use of exclusionary practices and school climate in high schools, and Chapter 5 includes similar information about middle grade schools. To measure teacher and student perceptions of climate, UChicago CCSR has been partnering with CPS to survey all students in grades 6-12 and all teachers across the district since the early 1990s. This survey, entitled *My Voice, My School,* was administered annually from 2011 through 2014 and every other year prior to that. Sets of questions were combined into measures of general concepts using Rasch analysis. The concepts we focus on in this report are teacher perceptions of crime and disorder and student perceptions of the quality of peer relationships. The items included in these measures are reported in **Table C.1**.

Sometimes survey information is seen as subjective. However, there is considerable evidence that these measures are valid instruments of school climate. One source of evidence comes from the strong correlation between students' and teachers' reports of safety and disorder in their schools, even though they come from different sources of information. The relationship of teacher reports of safety with student reports of safety is stronger than the relationship of either with characteristics of the students or neighborhoods they serve, such as crime and poverty.

TABLE C.1

Survey Question Wording

Survey Measure	Survey Questions
Safety (Student)	How safe do you feel: 1. Outside around the school? 2. Traveling between home and school? 3. In the hallways and bathrooms of the school? 4. In your classes? ***Not Safe, Somewhat Safe, Mostly Safe, Very Safe***
Crime and Disorder (Teacher)	To what extent is each of the following a problem at your school?: 1. Physical conflicts among students. 2. Robbery or theft 3. Gang activity 4. Disorder in classrooms 5. Disorder in hallways 6. Student disrespect of teachers 7. Threats of violence toward teachers ***Not at All, A Little, Some, To a Great Extent***
Teacher-Student Trust (Student)	How much do you agree with: 1. My teachers really care about me 2. My teachers always keep his/her promises 3. My teachers always try to be fair 4. I feel safe and comfortable with my teachers at this school 5. When my teachers tell me not to do something, I know he/she has a good reason 6. My teachers will always listen to students' ideas 7. My teachers treat me with respect ***Strongly Disagree, Disagree, Agree, Strongly Agree***

Survey Measure	Survey Questions
Student Responsibility (Teacher)	How many of the students in your [TARGET] class: 1. Come to class on time? 2. Attend class regularly? 3. Come to class prepared with the appropriate supplies and books? 4. Regularly pay attention in class? 5. Actively participate in class activities? 6. Always turn in their homework? ***None, Some, About Half, Most, Nearly All***
Course Clarity (Student)	How much do you agree with the following statements about your [TARGET] class: 1. I learn a lot from feedback on my work. 2. It's clear to me what I need to do to get a good grade. 3. The work we do in class is good preparation for the test. 4. The homework assignments help me to learn the course material. 5. I know what my teacher wants me to learn in this class. ***Strongly Disagree, Disagree, Agree, Strongly Agree***
Academic Personalism (Student)	The teacher for your [target] class: 1. Helps me catch up if I am behind. 2. Is willing to give extra help on schoolwork if I need it. 3. Notices if I have trouble learning something. 4. Gives me specific suggestions about how I can improve my work in this class. 5. Explains things in a different way if I don't understand something in class. ***Strongly Disagree, Disagree, Agree, Strongly Agree***
Academic Press (Student)	How much do you agree with?: 1. This class really makes me think. 2. I'm really learning a lot in this class. 3. My teacher expects everyone to work hard. 4. My teacher expects me to do my best all the time 5. My teacher wants us to become better thinkers, not just memorize things. ***Strongly Disagree, Disagree, Agree, Strongly Agree*** In your class, how often: 1. Are you challenged? 2. Do you have to work hard to do well? 3. Does the teacher ask difficult questions on tests? 4. Does the teacher ask difficult questions in class ***Never, Once In a While, Most of the Time, All the Time***
Peer Relationships (Student)	How much do you agree with the following statements about students in your school? Most students in my school: 1. Like to put each other down. 2. Help each other learn. 3. Don't get along together very well. 4. Treat each other with respect. ***Strongly Disagree, Disagree, Agree, Strongly Agree***
Quality of Student Discussion (Teacher)	To what extent do the following characteristics describe discussions that occur in your [TARGET] class: 1. Students build on each other's ideas during discussion. 2. Students use data and text references to support their ideas. 3. Students show each other respect. 4. Students provide constructive feedback to their peers/teachers. 5. Most students participate in the discussion at some point. ***Never, Rarely, Sometimes, Almost Always***

Appendix D
Methods for Categorizing Schools' Use of Exclusionary Discipline Practices

In Chapter 2, we introduced three elementary school and three high school groups based on the degree to which they used exclusionary disciplinary practices. Groups were created using principal component analysis (PCA). PCA is a way to reduce the dimensionality of the data. In this case, we have multiple measures of how schools use suspensions and police, and we want to put that information together to construct a single measure of the school's reliance on exclusionary practices.

We included various measures of suspension usage and police contact in the analysis, specifically percent of students at a school who received an ISS, percent of students at a school who received an OSS, percent of students at a school who were involved in an incident that resulted in their arrest, suspensions (ISS and OSS) per capita, whether or not any students at the school were involved in an incident that required police contact (as defined in the CPS student code of conduct), and schools' over or under reliance on police (constructed by dividing the total number of incidents that require police contact by the number of times police were actually contacted by the school—a value less than one indicates the school is contacting police less often than required, and a value greater than one means the school contacted the police more often than required).

PCA places different weights on these variables and combines them into a single measure, called a component, in a way that best explains the underlying variance of the data. We take the first principal component, which is a continuous variable that ranks schools, generated from the analysis to group schools together based on how they use exclusionary practices. The components themselves are continuous variables. We created the cutpoints for the different exclusionary discipline practice (EDP) groups by identifying natural breaks in this underlying continuous variable. We ran this analysis separately for elementary and high schools.

Appendix E

Methods for Analyzing the Effects of Reducing Suspension Length

We find that, descriptively, there is a negative relationship between school-level suspension rates and climate, as shown in Chapter 3. This relationship exists even when controlling for characteristics of the students the school serves, including racial/ethnic and gender composition, percent of students with an identified disability, incoming achievement, neighborhood poverty, and school size. **Table E.1** shows the coefficients from a regression of the school climate as an outcome on the EDP groups (with the low EDP schools as the omitted category) and the school-level characteristics described. It includes the estimates shown in **Table 8** in Chapter 5 for middle grades and compares those estimates to the high school results.

The coefficients in **Table E.1** can still be subject to bias if there is an unobserved factor that influences a school's use of exclusionary discipline practices and school climate. It is also hard to establish the direction of causality when trying to determine the relationship between school culture and the use of exclusionary practices—does the use of suspensions cause worse climates, or do schools with negative climates use more suspensions because they have so many behavioral problems? In the summer of 2012, district policy regarding the length of suspensions changed—mandatory 10-day suspensions for certain violations were removed from the Student Code of Conduct (SCC) and schools were required to attain district permission to suspend students for longer than five days for a single incident. This policy change led to a sudden change in the number of days students in high school were suspended, allowing us to identify the effect of reducing the length of suspensions on student outcomes and school climate.

The analysis focuses on high schools, since it was rare for students in the middle grades to receive long suspensions even before the policy. The teacher analyses examine all teachers in the school. The student analyses only examine outcomes among ninth-graders, comparing students who entered high school before and after the policy.

TABLE E.1

School Climate and Instructional Quality by EDP Use in High Schools

School Climate Measure	High Schools	
	Medium EDP Compared to Low EDP	High EDP Compared to Low DEP
Learning Climate		
Safety	-0.334*	-0.334
Crime and Disorder (positive is worse)	0.505***	0.522***
Teacher-Student Trust	-0.210	-0.275
Student Responsibility	-0.407**	-0.914***
Instructional Quality		
Course Clarity	-0.274	-0.417*
Academic Personalism	-0.055	-0.139
Academic Press	-0.174	-0.195
Peer Relationships	-0.440***	-0.373***
Quality of Student Discussion	-0.364*	-0.322

Note: The coefficients shown in this table are from a regression of a particular school climate measure on the percent of students who are African American, Latino, special education, and male, as well as the average poverty level of the neighborhoods where students live, incoming achievement, and student enrollment. An omitted group is the low EDP schools, so the coefficients shown are in reference to reported school climate at that group of schools. Survey measures are standardized, so the coefficients represent differences from low EDP schools in standard deviation units. Asterisks denote statistical significance: *** at the 0.01 level, ** at the 0.05 level, and * at the 0.10 level.

We focus on ninth-graders so that their responses about school climate are not affected by prior years' experiences in the school, and so that the analysis of achievement is based on the same set of assessments for the entire analytic sample. Students at older grades also are at a much higher risk of school dropout and high absence rates associated with school disengagement than first-time ninth-graders, so we limit the analysis to ninth-graders to avoid problems of sample attrition for these reasons. We look at policy effects among all ninth-graders, not just those students who were suspended. Doing the analysis in that way allows us to say how reducing the length of suspensions affects the overall climate and degree of learning.

Data come from two pre- and two post-policy years, spanning 2010-11 to 2013-14. We implement a difference-in-difference model with school fixed effects, comparing the same schools to themselves before and after the policy change. We include a variety of control variables, so we are comparing similar students in terms of demographics, poverty, special needs, and prior disciplinary history who attend the same school. We also control for changes in school suspension rates over time (i.e., the percentage of students who were suspended each year). The framework is reduced form in nature, so we look directly at the effect of being in a post-policy year on student and school outcomes.

Specifically, the student-level regression model is shown as equation 1:

$$(1)\ Y_{itj} = Y^1_{ij,\,t-1}\lambda + X^1_{ijt}\beta + 1[t > 2011](\theta_1 + \theta_2 d_{j2011}) + \mu_j + \varepsilon_{ijt}$$

where Y is an outcome for student *i* in school *j* in year *t*. The set of student-level outcomes included in this report are math and reading test scores, attendance, students' reports of safety and peer relationships in the school and teachers' reports of crime and disorder in the school. There is a vector of student controls **X** described above. There is an indicator variable for the post-reform period, $1[t > 2011]$, that equals 1 in 2012-13 and 2013-14 and 0 for years prior to the policy change. This specification allows for an intercept shift in the outcome post-policy denoted by θ_1. The interaction of the indicator with d_{jt} allows the policy to have a differential effect for schools with different rates of long suspension usage prior to the policy. This means that the estimation equation will allow for schools where long suspensions were used more frequently pre-policy to be affected differently than schools that used long suspensions less often prior to the policy change. The school fixed effects are μ_j, which restricts the identification of the post-policy effects on outcomes to within school comparisons. A random error term is also included.

To look at the effect of reducing suspensions on school climate, we apply the same estimation framework but outcomes and control variables are measured at the school-level. This is equation 2. Instead of student covariates, we include characteristics of the student body. School-level outcomes presented in this report include teacher reports of crime and disorder and student reports of the quality of peer relationships.

$$(2)\ \bar{Y}_{itj} = Y^1_{j,\,t-1}\lambda + \bar{X}^1_{jt}\beta + 1[t > 2011](\theta_1 + \theta_2 d_{j2011}) + \mu_j + \bar{\varepsilon}_{ij}$$

The results shown in **Table 3 on p.31** in the main text of this report are $\bar{\theta}_2$ multiplied by two different values for d_{j2011}. We first look at $d_{j2011} = 0.04$, which means that 4 percent of students in the school received a long OSS the year prior to the policy. This was the average rate of long OSS in 2011-12 (**see Figure 10 on p.30**), and represents the change in outcomes due to the policy at the typical school. We also present $d_{j2011} = 0.10$, or a school where 10 percent of students received a long OSS prior to the policy, which is representative for schools where many students are suspended for over a week prior to the policy.

This analysis is part of a larger paper looking at the effects of the suspension length reduction policy in CPS. This paper also shows the effects separately for students who were at high and low risk of receiving a long suspension. The working paper can be accessed from the UChicago CCSR website.[31]

31 Mader, Sartain, & Steinberg (2015).

Appendix F

Methods for Analyzing the Effects of Supplemental Practices

In Chapter 4, we offer evidence that use of supplemental practices is correlated school climate in high schools. In particular, we find that for low and moderate exclusionary practice schools (EDP), percentage of suspension incidents that were accompanied by supplemental corresponded to better reports of student and teacher reports of climate in their school, but in high EDP schools, the opposite relationship is found.

We used partial correlation analyses in order to examine these relationships. The r^2 statistic and significance level for each relevant comparison is given in **Table 6 on p.41**.

In our analyses, we restrict data to high schools, following the greater reliance on suspensions in high school, and the precedent of earlier chapters. We further restrict data to those high schools that gave at least ten suspensions, and for which we have measurement of all variables in both the 2012-13 and 2013-14 school years. The variables of interest were the extent to which schools used supplemental practices and school climate measures. The extent to which schools used any supplemental practice was operationalized as the percentage of incidents in which a suspension was paired with a parent conference, restorative justice practice, individualized intervention, or other practice (**see Appendix B** for a full list of these practices). A combination of practices for any single incident was counted only once in the any supplemental practices category. The extent to which schools used restorative justice or parent conference practices was calculated as the percentage of suspension incidents that were paired with a restorative justice practice or parent conference, respectively. Climate measures included student reports of safety and peer relationships, and teacher reports of crime and disorder. They are taken from the annual *My Voice, My School* survey administered to Chicago Public Schools. **Appendix C** has a full description of the items that make up these measures. Rasch scores are produced from survey measures, then aggregated to the school-level.

Control variables used in the analysis were school-level measures. Control variables, listed exhaustively, are as follows: Racial composition, suspension rates, school enrollment (log transformed), average student incoming achievement, and students' average neighborhood poverty. In addition, when extent of parent conference (restorative practices) use was of interest, the use of restorative justice practices (parent conferences) was used as a control. Values of all variables (x, y, and controls) used in the analyses are calculated by first standardizing across two years of data (2012-13 and 2013-14), and then averaging across those values in order to reduce measurement error.

Analyses using restorative justice practices as a predictor are not reported for low EDP schools. Restorative practices varied little in these schools, making the relationship between these practices and safety subject to the effects of a few marginal outliers. While the relationship between restorative justice practices and students reports of climate was consistent with the other findings here, we do not report them given the lack of variation in the use of restorative practices. Restorative practices in medium and high EDP schools varied, but were positively skewed. Log transforming these variables improved the normality of the distribution and did not change the pattern of results, nor the significance level for any analysis. Analyses are reported with untransformed variables.

A second analysis used HLM to evaluate the extent to which changes in supplemental practice use from the 2012-13 school year to the 2013-14 years predicted changes in student reports of safety, student reports of peer relationship, and teacher reports of crime and disorder, controlling for racial composition, suspension rates, school enrollment, incoming achievement, and neighborhood poverty.

The observation level regression model is shown as equation 1:

$$(1)\ Y_{itj} = \beta_{0i} + \delta \mathit{Supplemental\ Practices}_{it} + X^1_{it}\beta + \mu_t + \varepsilon_{it}$$

$$(2)\ \beta_{0i} = \gamma_{00} + \mu_{it}$$

where Y is a climate outcome for school *i* in year *t*, the **X** vector includes school-level characteristics, and μ_t is a year fixed effect. The coefficient of interest is the estimate of δ, which is the association of climate and a school's use of supplemental practices (percent of total suspension incidents accompanied by supplemental practice). The HLM analyses revealed no significant effects or interactions.

ABOUT THE AUTHORS

LAUREN SARTAIN is a Senior Research Analyst at UChicago CCSR. She has a bachelor's degree from the University of Texas at Austin, as well as a master's degree and PhD in public policy from the Harris School at the University of Chicago. She has worked at Chapin Hall and the Federal Reserve Bank of Chicago. Sartain's research interests include principal and teacher quality, school choice, and urban school reform.

ELAINE M. ALLENSWORTH is the Lewis-Sebring Director at UChicago CCSR where she has conducted research on educational policy for the last 15 years. She is best known for her studies of high school graduation and college readiness, and also conducts research in the areas of school leadership and school organization. Her work on early indicators of high school graduation has been adopted for tracking systems used in Chicago and other districts across the country. She is one of the authors of the book *Organizing Schools for Improvement: Lessons from Chicago*, which provides a detailed analysis of school practices and community conditions that promote school improvement. Allensworth holds a PhD in sociology and an MA in urban studies from Michigan State University. She was once a high school Spanish and science teacher.

SHANETTE PORTER is a Senior Research Analyst at UChicago CCSR. Her current research focuses on the impact of policy change on school approaches and outcomes, as well as the role of social, emotional, and motivational factors in predicting student outcomes. Prior to joining UChicago CCSR, Porter completed a postdoctoral fellowship, jointly appointed at Northwestern University's Institute for Policy Research and the Department of Psychology. Her fellowship work focused on the cognitive-behavioral dynamics of intergroup interactions. Porter received her PhD in social and personality psychology from Cornell University, her MA in industrial-organizational psychology from Michigan State University, and her BA in psychology from Yale University.

www.ingramcontent.com/pod-product-compliance
Lightning Source LLC
Chambersburg PA
CBHW042016080426
42735CB00002B/69

* 9 7 8 0 9 9 0 9 5 6 3 5 8 *